LIVE
TO
RIDE

LIVE TO RIDE

Finding Joy and Meaning on a Bicycle

Peter Flax

Principal photography by Jered & Ashley Gruber
and John Watson

Artisan Books | New York, NY

Library of Congress Cataloging-in-Publication Data

Names: Flax, Peter, author.
Title: Live to ride : finding joy and meaning on a bicycle / Peter Flax.
Description: New York : Artisan Books, 2024. | Includes index.
Identifiers: LCCN 2023029031 | ISBN 9781648291319 (hardback)
Subjects: LCSH: Cycling—Psychological aspects.
Classification: LCC GV1041 .F58 2024 | DDC 796.601/9—dc23/eng/20230802
LC record available at https://lccn.loc.gov/2023029031

Design by Su Barber

Artisan books may be purchased in bulk for business, educational, or promotional use. For information, please contact your local bookseller or the Hachette Book Group Special Markets Department at special.markets@hbgusa.com.

The publisher is not responsible for websites (or their content) that are not owned by the publisher.

The Hachette Speakers Bureau provides a wide range of authors for speaking events. To find out more, go to hachettespeakersbureau.com or email HachetteSpeakers@hbgusa.com.

Published by Artisan,
an imprint of Workman Publishing,
a division of Hachette Book Group, Inc.
1290 Avenue of the Americas
New York, NY 10104
artisanbooks.com

The Artisan name and logo are registered trademarks of Hachette Book Group, Inc.

Printed in China on responsibly sourced paper
First printing, February 2024

10 9 8 7 6 5 4 3 2 1

To my sons, Lucas and Roscoe

A participant in New York's vibrant Bike Life scene, a rider who calls himself Latti Datti showcases his skill and verve with the Manhattan Bridge looming in the background.

CONTENTS

INTRODUCTION

I am a bike rider. If you're reading this, I'm guessing you are, too. I don't think of my bike life as a hobby or a fitness routine or a leisure activity. My connection to riding is far deeper. And though it could be accurately characterized as a lifestyle, that term has been hijacked in this era to describe something that can be distilled into an Instagram post or leveraged in a marketing campaign. For me, riding is something that truly shapes my identity—how I look at the universe, how I center myself in a complicated world, how I find joy and meaning and, often, very good cups of coffee. If you are a bike rider, I bet you understand what I mean.

For many decades, bike culture has slotted most of us into tribes. This is true even if you never realized that you'd been categorized. There is no simple way to opt out.

Some of the subcultures are obvious. There are the roadies, with shaved legs, spandex kits, and carbon fiber race bikes. There are the mountain bikers, with baggy shorts and full-suspension rigs, who then fall into a grab bag of off-road subcategories to separate the lift-served downhillers from the cross-country purists and enduro fun seekers. There are the commuters, who often have sturdy bikes, hard-core rain gear, and a purpose-driven lifestyle. There are the century fanatics and tourers and triathletes and beach cruisers and bikepackers and messenger types and errand runners. There are packs of wheelie kids, folks who prefer recumbents or tandems, collectors of vintage gear. Each group has distinctive equipment and apparel. The groups have long operated like a giant caste system for people who pedal, complete with subcultural rules and hierarchies and historical tensions.

I know all about the inner workings of this subcultural universe because I participated in it for thirty-plus years—first as a disinterested subject, then as a loyal adherent, and eventually as a kind of gatekeeper. For much of that time, I pursued riding as if there was something to be mastered, many layers of nuance to be peeled back and understood in order to glimpse and reach the core. This quest impacted many aspects of my life—how I ate and trained, what length socks I purchased, how I did seemingly important little things like leaning on my handlebars in a parking lot or snapping photos of a bicycle to share on social media. It was as though I were on a quest to become a more authentic cyclist

The author in 2013. This photograph accompanied an editor's note that he wrote in his role as editor in chief of *Bicycling* magazine.

9

The best thing for every bike rider is lots more bike riders. There is transformative power on the table if bike culture can unite—the power to make riding more inclusive, safer, and even more fun.

who had earned membership in the inner circle. I acted like there was an unspoken code of conduct because there *was* an unspoken code of conduct.

Here's one example: I have been asked hundreds of times by outsiders why so many men who are passionate about riding road bikes shave their legs. I used to think it was a nettlesome question to answer, requiring a lengthy discourse on tradition, but I've changed my mind. If you are a serious bike racer, there are a bunch of logical, granular reasons to shave your legs—it's better for massage and simplifies wound care, it makes it easier to apply warming embrocation in inclement weather, and it imparts a small but real aerodynamic advantage. But the real reason most road riders, whether they race or not, do it is to belong—to tell themselves and other riders and random people in their life that they are serious enough to present to the world with shaved legs and a weird tan. (It's worth noting, perhaps, that most women who ride are able to sidestep this arguably silly tradition because they are bound by other arguably silly traditions.)

Learning to ride a bicycle is actually quite simple—something that can be accomplished in an afternoon—but figuring out how to fully embed yourself in some cycling subcultures can take years or even decades. Hundreds of thousands of bike riders have embarked on this journey, but it has been a little different for me because I am a writer and editor who has worked in this space. I ultimately became the editor in chief of *Bicycling*, the world's largest magazine for cycling enthusiasts, and in this role was something like a spokesperson or bellwether for the culture. I had a professional mission to help riders become more competent and educated, to help people get faster and fitter and better equipped. I already was clued in to the profound nature of bicycles—how these machines and people's love for them were connected to existential matters—but I didn't yet understand the shortcomings of compartmentalizing this amazing universe into subcultures. Even though I didn't really understand mountain bike culture and made a lot of jokes about triathletes—as if people wearing short socks, using aerobars, and marking numbers on their shoulders is funnier than roadies wearing brightly colored spandex and slathering chamois cream on their intimate bits—I thought all the subcultures were cool. I even green-lit a pretty humorous book called *Bike Tribes* that codified the major subcultures like a field guide.

In short, I thought there was an inevitability and a logic to all these subcultures full of enthusiasts striving for excellence among their own. I honestly questioned whether the roadies and the commuters and the triathletes wanted to hang out together.

But a lot has changed for me in the past decade. In 2014, I left that job at the big bike magazine and moved from Pennsylvania to Los Angeles. My professional life and riding life and, I guess, the rest of my life were transformed. I got a job at the *Hollywood Reporter*, started commuting by bike in LA, and struggled to figure out what my role in bike culture would become. I was no longer employed as an authority on the matter.

Moving from a bucolic exurb to the most populous county in America, a sprawling and eternally sunny place where nearly every ride is a perilous cosmic adventure, turned my riding life upside down. On my long daily commutes, I would pedal alongside professional athletes and restaurant workers and travel through both the beautiful splendor and the bleaker sides of the city. On the beachfront bike path near my home, I noticed that one group of riders would say hi to me when I was on a race bike in spandex and that an entirely different demographic that had ignored me the day before would acknowledge me if I rode an upright bike in jeans. I saw sporty riders and affluent casual riders fighting bike-lane projects that would benefit utility riders. I met a lot of mountain bikers who had stopped riding on the road because they were afraid of getting hit. I went on large, fast group rides with strangers who accepted me because I looked the part. I suppose I suddenly felt adjacent to many subcultures without truly belonging to any of them.

At the same time, outside forces were radically changing bike culture, too. New kinds of bikes—like gravel bikes, which meld qualities of a good road bike with those of a good mountain bike, and electric bikes—began inspiring more riders to step outside of their niches. US cities both big and small were being reshaped, with an influx of younger riders, tons of new infrastructure, and an explosion of bike-share programs—all things that transformed urban riding from a hearty subculture into a legitimate cultural phenomenon with way more women and people of color involved. In fashion magazines and retail environments, I saw more and more bicycles being used as objects to connote the good life and to convey a kind of distinctive personal style. For the first time since the 1970s, there was a legitimate bike boom—this sense that the bicycle could truly revolutionize cities and the world.

Across the board, I saw change everywhere I looked. I saw professional bike racers getting involved in advocacy, I saw New Yorkers in business attire riding to the office on a Citi Bike, I saw everyone parking every manner of bicycle outside America's coffee shops, I saw people from different corners of the bike universe talking to one another on Twitter (in the pre-Musk era). All this change had been put in motion before the pandemic, but Covid-19 was like a spark that helped the bike boom catch fire. Suddenly,

streets were quieter and gyms were closed and people sought new ways to get active, and what followed was an unprecedented explosion of consumer interest in bicycles. I saw a lot of things that struck me as an opportunity—an opportunity for bicycles to occupy a larger place in our culture and our cities and the public consciousness.

This is when I truly started to realize that the hierarchical nature of bike culture would hold us back. A huge number of bike enthusiasts, myself included, have been indoctrinated in this idea that they're part of a community that's shaped like a pyramid—with clueless beginners at the bottom and professional racers at the top. There's a website called Velominati—it's worth mentioning that it began around 2009 as an inside joke—that gained a passionate following for codifying all the "rules" of road cycling, or, in simplistic terms, how to act like a pro even if you're not. At last count, there were ninety-five rules (the final one being to never lift your bicycle over your head unless you are using a roof rack on a car).

What started as a joke became something else. In my experience, people who love bikes are passionate and smart and interesting, but they tend to be a relatively earnest bunch. Too many riders took the rules—whether offered by the "keepers" of the Velominati rules or paraphrased by the editors of enthusiast magazines like the one I had run—too seriously, which perpetuated the social order that I was beginning to question.

For bike culture to reach its full potential, everyone needs to feel welcome. Cycling should not seem intimidating to newcomers. It should not take years to feel like a real cyclist. I spent a long time thinking and writing about this, and in the end, the best piece of counterpropaganda I could think of was this: If you're riding a bike, you're doing it right.

This mantra has led me to the central theme of this book: There is *way* more that connects everyone who rides a bike than there is that divides us. Presuming you're not bullying pedestrians, we're all unified by a love for some universal ideas that transcend what kind of bike or tires or clothing we're outfitted with while we're pedaling. I'm aspiring to supplant the old way of thinking—to undermine the paradigm of bike tribes and all those prescriptive rules—and instead find new and compelling ways to unify bike culture as the big happy family it should be.

The recent boom in gravel riding has brought road riders and mountain bike lovers together into a beautiful and welcoming community.

This is what I've spent more than a year contemplating: Why do we ride? What, exactly, unifies us?

From the beginning, people who ride bikes have been fervent outsiders of sorts. Soon after a young German named Karl Drais invented his Laufmaschine, a wooden precursor of the bicycle, in 1817, the world's first bike craze began. And within a few years, big cities like Milan, London, New York, and Paris had banned the contraption. This history, which is still being reenacted two centuries later, is something that connects us—people who love to ride are united by a common passion but wind up misunderstood and often vilified by those who don't love to ride.

Bike culture is in so many ways defined by this yin and yang—the interplay between the light of our passion and the dark forces that make riding more isolating, more stigmatizing, and frankly more dangerous than it needs to be. This book is not a straightforward manual of bike advocacy—there's no prescriptive advice for making riding safer or polemics on why bike culture is so often maligned by outsiders. It's more of a celebratory work of covert advocacy, founded on my confidence that many positive things will happen as everyone who rides absorbs and accepts the interconnectedness we share. The best thing for every bike rider is lots more bike riders. There is transformative power on the table if bike culture can unite—the power to make riding more inclusive, safer, and even more fun.

Each of the following chapters—Adventure, Speed, Utility, Nature, Competition, and Self-Expression—explores a quality that explains why we ride. The sum of my life's experience is that most riders highly value most of these qualities. And that way more than by our choice of equipment or apparel, our identity as riders is shaped by these profound commonalities. They are the glue that holds us together.

This might sound esoteric at first, but for me, it is quite pragmatic and emotional. Now, as I ride around Los Angeles, I feel that everyone on a bike is like family. The restaurant workers who wash dishes until 1:00 a.m. and then ride home, the venture capitalists on 14-pound (6.3 kg) Italian race bikes, kids heading to the beach with surfboards on a bike rack, folks slow-rolling to yoga class, graybeards on recumbents with flags flapping in the wind, the fixie kids and the wheelie kids and the BMX kids—everyone is family. This is such a powerful feeling that I want to share it with everyone who rides.

Ask yourself why you ride. No matter what kind of bikes you own or what you wear when you ride, I bet you have some common aspirations. To test yourself and find yourself and express yourself. To find some peace and beauty. To inject fun and adventure into your busy life. To get where you need to go—especially if the journey involves coffee.

People who ride know that the bicycle is one of the greatest inventions in human history. It's a machine that can transport you—whether toward the fulfillment of a physical goal or to a geographic destination or on an existential journey. And we are on the cusp of having our broader culture accept how bicycles can change the world for the better. Now is not the time to isolate ourselves in smaller communities that sanctify our differences—now is the time to stand together and share the profound strengths of our common ground.

I am a bike rider. If you're nodding your head right now, I'm certain you are a bike rider, too.

Curly, a New Yorker who did her first wheelie in 2017, is now a mainstay in the city's Bike Life culture. To fully appreciate her passion, check out @curlybloxks on Instagram.

ADVENTURE

Most adults live dependably structured lives, defined in large part by schedules and plans and obligations. The raw spontaneity that so many of us enjoyed as children or teenagers can get tougher and tougher to access, especially now that we're tethered to technology nearly every waking moment. The truth is, our sense of adventure can be dulled or repressed by modern life.

But as so many riders know, a bike ride can change everything. In a literal sense, a bicycle can transport you to places you want to go—to your school or office, to the summit of a local hill, to some fitness objective—but it can do more than that. A bicycle can also transport you to an entirely different mindset, a realm where you can embrace the unexpected and live in the moment.

The bicycle is so many things—a highly efficient mode of transport, a sophisticated piece of sporting equipment, an object of beauty and expression, a refined toy for thrill seekers—yet it also is a wondrous time machine, able to help us recapture the joys of improvisation and discovery as if we were children again. People who ride a lot know this is true and also that it can somehow happen during a one-hour loop. And when you tackle an all-day ride or something even more ambitious than that, the odds of being rewarded with a transformative adventure are extremely high.

Within bike culture, I see more appreciation for the value of this kind of exploration. I see it as exponentially more riders seek unpaved adventures or get into touring. I see it as more bike racers—even those in the pro ranks—pivot from purely structured

Riders understand that pedaling down unfamiliar roads can transport you to a more meaningful state of mind.

goals and traditional races to experiential challenges through gravel riding, bikepacking, and alternative events. I see it as more people explore their city with a bike and a flexible itinerary.

In my lifetime of riding, I have been on thousands of small adventures but only one truly massive one. In 1992, I rode cross-country, from Seattle to New York, with my best friend, Dave. I still hope to tackle another adventure of that scale in my life, but even if not, the experience changed me forever by opening my eyes to where a bicycle could take me. It's no exaggeration to say that the trip permanently altered my sense of possibility. I think people who get serious about yoga or meditation or long-distance hiking have similar realizations as they see something they began as a physical pursuit wind up having metaphysical components.

There was one evening on our trip, about a week into the long journey, when Dave and I were setting up our tent and were surprised by a guy with a shotgun. Dave and I had been halfway up Wauconda Pass in eastern Washington when one of us broke a spoke, and with darkness looming, we decided to call it a day. That little grassy patch next to a horse pasture, without a house in sight, seemed like the perfect place to crash—but the bearded veteran who lived at the end of the driveway disagreed.

"You boys horse rustlers?" he demanded, shining a heavy-duty flashlight in our eyes. We were standing there in spandex shorts with tent poles in our hands; our fully loaded touring bikes leaned against the pasture fence.

The situation deescalated quickly. Fifteen minutes later, we were in his living room swapping stories as we sipped whiskey-spiked coffee. He told us about the leg injury he brought home from Vietnam and his one-man war against horse thieves. Dave and I described the first week of our summer adventure. This was more than twenty-five years ago.

Contemplations about how the experience would age over the decades were the furthest thing from my mind. I was as rooted in the present as I'd ever been in my life. Dave and I averaged seven or eight hours a day on our bikes, with long stretches on alpine mountain passes or into a High Plains headwind. There was a lot of time to daydream and spin circles and suffer. We ate four or five square meals a day—a mountain of grilled cheese sandwiches and vanilla milkshakes and Hostess fruit pies. Clif Bars weren't on the market yet. In the same vein, nobody had even imagined the word *bikepacking*.

For much of the trip, we traced a route recommended by a nonprofit group called Bikecentennial (it would soon rebrand itself as the less-evocative Adventure Cycling Association). Back in 1976, Bikecentennial had introduced the idea of bike touring to American society with a massive cross-country ride organized to celebrate the nation's two hundredth birthday.

After a few weeks on the road, Dave and I began living a new reality. Once you truly settle into an adventure, strange and wondrous things start to happen. You see the randomness in the universe, you open yourself to strangers, you lose a sense

The author, somewhere in Montana, during the summer of 1992 on a cross-country ride that remains the biggest adventure of his life.

Two riders soak in the view of the Los Angeles skyline from the Griffith Park helipad, an iconic spot to pause during rambles through the park.

Once you truly settle into an adventure, strange and wondrous things start to happen. You see the randomness in the universe, you open yourself to strangers, you lose a sense of anything beyond the present moment.

of anything beyond the present moment. Things that otherwise would seem bizarre—like the night we slept in a jail cell on the reservation of the Spirit Lake Dakota tribe, or the time I almost hit a porcupine while descending a mountain pass in Glacier National Park in the dark—seem normal.

This trip undoubtedly was the greatest adventure of my life. For an entire summer, I was on the move, passing through beautiful places, testing my physical limits, soaking in all the unpredictable joys of being in the moment. It was just me and my friend and my bike and this profound sense of freedom. Everything about the experience felt larger than life—I mean, we pedaled more than 3,000 miles (4,800 km)!

But in the intervening three decades, I've learned that I can recapture the spirit of that grand adventure in bite-size portions in my riding life. My existence now is considerably more complicated than it was then—defined by obligations to my family and work—but I've continued to pursue the unknown and the joy of discovery on the bike. This is something that nearly everyone who rides a bicycle can relate to. So many riders can still remember that feeling of being a kid on a bike, of exploring their neighborhood and the freedom of prospecting new territory. Like so many magical things about riding bikes, this feeling is surprisingly easy to replicate as an adult.

People who ride a lot—whether to get around the city or to get lost on quiet trails or for fitness—are unified by an appreciation of this feeling. They know that even a leisurely ten-minute ride to the post office or smoothie joint often has an undeniable experiential quality. They know that pedaling through the most familiar places frequently brings unexpected delights—and that turning down new roads can be low-key thrilling. Our minds are open to appreciate surprises, primed to actually seek out experiences that are a little weird or unnerving. I have absolutely no criticism for folks who love to ride indoors—I get it—but I think that riding outside exposes you to modest adventures that can enrich your life in a big way.

It certainly has enriched mine. For eleven years, I lived in Pennsylvania's Lehigh Valley, as close to a cycling paradise as anywhere in the world I've ever been. On long weekend rambles, I'd head north or west, through Mennonite farm country or toward

Riding through unfamiliar territory can put you in a playful headspace that evokes the freedom that many of us first tasted as kids.

the foothills of the Pocono Mountains. That part of the Keystone State is a seemingly endless lattice of country roads, with noticeably different weather in each of the four seasons. If I wandered for a few hours, I'd eventually wind up on a gravel road or steep forested climb I'd never tackled before. On those stretches, I'd feel this bristling energy that was the excitement of discovery. I'd come home from those rides transformed, back in suburbia with chores on my plate but satisfied in some existential way.

These days, I call Los Angeles home, and my riding life is mostly defined by commuting to work. There are no quiet rides by cornfields anymore. I haven't seen a gangly fawn or been chased by a dog in years. But the thirst for adventure on the bike has hardly gone away—it has simply changed shape.

For about four years, I worked at the *Hollywood Reporter* and commuted by bike from my home in Manhattan Beach to their offices in LA's Mid-City neighborhood. I covered more than 30,000 miles (48,000 km) doing a pretty repetitive route—pedaling on an oceanfront beach path, then on a grittier bike path along one of LA's concrete riverbeds, followed by twenty-five minutes of prototypically hairy urban riding. In a way I didn't foresee, this new kind of riding was as stimulating and unpredictable as anything I'd done before on a bike.

I got pummeled by winter storms along the beach. I smelled the taco trucks. I learned how urban riding was like technical mountain biking—where you have to be hyperalert to all the hazards that could ruin a ride. I saw the depths of the city tucked out of sight to most under every bridge. I often rode home after midnight, when the only other people in the bike lanes were restaurant workers heading east after a long day. In short, I got to be part of the chaotic fabric of Los Angeles. When I arrived at the office or back home, I sometimes felt tired, but I always felt so *alive*. While most everyone else in LA was slowly dying in a horrible motor vehicle commute, I was a supporting actor in this cinematic saga.

It took a couple of years of this new routine for me to truly realize how deeply this riding was satisfying my elemental desire for adventure. And I started thinking about how it was fulfilling a central part of my life on a bike—transporting me literally as it transported me out of the ordinary. I really needed the bike to take me places beyond my physical destination.

Pro racer turned epic adventurer Svein Tuft (see page 35)—who does rides tougher than my cross-country trek on a regular basis—describes his ramblings as an important "outlet" in his life. That word really resonates with me because it suggests that this kind of rolling discovery is at once an emotional release and an escape from the monotony and burdens of modern adult life. So often we begin and end our rides in the same place but return a slightly different person. We are, in all sorts of little and beautiful ways, changed by the journey. We ride to find things and to find ourselves.

I had absorbed this lesson in a profound way by the final night of my cross-country trip in 1992. Dave and I spent that night

Sometimes all it takes is an hour or two of exploration to get a taste of adventure that will change your state of mind.

Live to Ride

There's absolutely nothing wrong with riding indoors, but it can't really match the pure joy of rolling down quiet roads on a beautiful day with friends.

So often we begin and end our rides in the same place but return a slightly different person. We are, in all sorts of little and beautiful ways, changed by the journey. We ride to find things and to find ourselves.

in Bear Mountain State Park, only 40 miles (64 km) from our childhood homes in New York. We stumbled onto a cluster of unoccupied cabins that surrounded a small meadow, and one of them was unlocked. We cooked one last spaghetti dinner on the deck and then slept on the saggy cots inside.

In the middle of the night, I woke up and crept outside to pee. I stared at my feet as I shuffled to the edge of the meadow. And then, when I finally looked up, the meadow was awash in moonlight and full of deer that were staring at me. It was like a dream. I woke up Dave so he could see the dreamy deer, too.

In some respects, the whole trip was like a dream—at once otherworldly and yet so vivid. Something deeply personal and totally surprising. All feelings I would experience again, and still experience today when I get on my bike. Riding can enable a lifelong quest to find the unexpected, to be disconnected from our digital universe and plugged into the real world.

People who ride know that the intoxicating pleasures of adventure are boundless. It's not necessarily about suffering or heroic efforts or even about going far (though all of those things can eventually mutate into fun and a curious propensity for using the word *epic*). It's about being open to whatever comes your way. Bike riding can get you where you want to go—whether it's to the supermarket or a higher level of fitness or some quiet road two hours from home—and so often you realize that you've also reached a state of discovery. Maybe you got caught in a sudden thunderstorm or had a funny conversation with a stranger; perhaps you got temporarily lost or pushed yourself a little further than you anticipated. Maybe you set out on a tour to see a new area and found something new in yourself.

Rides can change us. A little adventure can strengthen us to tackle our obligations without being beholden to them, and they make our lives more interesting. I've come to recognize that it's an important reason why I ride—to get lost and found as I pedal through the world. Maybe you feel the same way.

We're better prepared to manage our responsibilities and digital obsessions after unplugging on a ride.

Live to Ride

Lachlan Morton

The Meaning of the Alt Tour

In the world of professional bike racing, there's no bigger event than the Tour de France. Nothing really comes close in terms of prestige and public interest. But during the summer of 2021, one pro racer's adventurous attempt to re-envision the tour attracted global attention.

On June 26, the same day the legendary three-week tour began, Australian racer Lachlan Morton rolled out of Brest to begin a self-supported epic ride he and his team called the Alt Tour. While his teammates and 176 other top pros embarked on twenty-one days of ultracompetitive individual race stages in various parts of France, Morton set out to ride the entire route with no support. Of course the pros in the race rode faster, but they slept in hotel rooms, got daily massages and chef-prepared meals, and were transferred in luxury buses from the end of each stage to the beginning of the next. By contrast, Morton slept in a tiny tent, bought and prepared his own food, carried his own gear, and pedaled the entire route.

"I thought of it as an homage to how the tour originally was, with really long days and riders on their own," says Morton, who already had a bunch of ultra-long-distance riding experience. "I was excited about the idea from the start but hadn't looked at the route at that point. When I really looked at the numbers, I realized that this was going to be the hardest thing I'd done by a significant margin. If you're after a quality experience, then you have to do something that makes you uncomfortable. You're forced to adapt as a person and an athlete."

Though Morton was riding daily mileages far beyond what most fit cyclists could dream of riding, his experiences weren't dissimilar to those of anyone on a long-distance bike tour. He stopped in small towns throughout France to fill up his water bottles and buy chocolate milk and bottles of beer and fresh-baked baguettes at local shops, he slept on the ground, he battled unexpected injuries, and he talked to tons of strangers. He also wrestled with loneliness and fatigue.

"To be honest, I've spent a lot of time racing in France, but that was the first time I really saw it," he says. "While you're racing, you only see these fragments. But this trip was like one big experience that never stopped."

Everywhere he went, Morton had short but memorable interactions with people he'd never met before and would never see again. "There's something about being on a bike," he says. "People are very welcoming. They can see you're tired or hungry. It brings out the best in people."

Not surprisingly, he had some genuinely rough moments. He had a bad flare-up of knee pain early in the trip—probably because a cleat on his shoe wasn't set up right—and so he went into a small department store in Brittany and bought a basic pair of sandals. The store wouldn't sell him a set of flat pedals, so he bought a cheap bike for seventy euros, removed the pedals, and gave the bike away at a campground. And for thousands of miles, the pro bike racer rode his race bike in sandals. It was the kind of improvisation an adventure requires.

Though he really wasn't motivated by the thrill of beating the peloton to Paris, the demands of this outsized enterprise pushed Morton to the limit. He recalls one huge day he had in the Alps—where he planned to ride 186 miles (300 km) and cross six mountain passes. "Man, that was hard," he recounts. "It was a really hot day, and I had blisters on my feet, and then I ran out of food around 4:00 p.m." He thought there was a small town with services near the campground he was staying at that night, but he was wrong. He wound up going to sleep hungry, knowing that he had to get up at 5:00 a.m. and climb two more mountain passes just to get breakfast.

But throughout his Alt Tour, he learned that adversity could hand out meaningful little gifts. "I had been dreading that morning ride, but it turned out to be great," Morton says. "I saw an amazing sunrise and had these beautiful roads through the Alps to myself. It was a reminder that many of the good things in life come from things that seem tough."

Early on July 13, in dark and rainy conditions, Morton rolled into Paris. He remembers saying "Holy shit" when he finally saw the Eiffel Tower. He completed the finishing circuit on the Champs-Élysées that the official Tour de

France competitors would race five days later. He had ridden a mind-boggling 3,423 miles (5,500 km)—1,300 miles (2,090 km) more than the tour covered—in eighteen days, climbing an equally astounding 219,000 feet (66,750 meters) of elevation along the way. He sat on the edge of the Champs and popped a huge bottle of Champagne, looking weary but triumphant.

Morton had not exactly been diddling much with his phone on his trip and didn't really understand how the public had become engaged with this huge undertaking. But tons of people—both hard-core bike-racing fans and folks who normally don't care about the Tour de France—tracked his progress and daily struggles online. His team, EF Education-Nippo, created a website to support the Alt Tour, and this site generated 618,000 page views during the tour, nearly triple what the team's regular site generated during the race.

"What Lachlan does inspires the imagination," says Jonathan Vaughters, the CEO and manager of Morton's team at the time. "His trip captured the spirit of the great adventure. It's why the original Tour de France in 1903 became a legend. It was an odyssey. That's about 180 degrees opposite from what most modern professional sports are. So what Lachlan did was recapture the epic nature of finishing something that hard."

And, Vaughters says, Morton's epic trip was relatable. "I think people can dream of doing what Lachlan does on some scale. It only takes extreme grit and determination," he says. "Riding a time-trial bike at the Tour de France also requires grit and determination, but it's harder to dream of because it takes 99.99 percent genetics."

In the end, Morton has happy memories of his epic trip rambling around France. He now tries to make every ride an adventure. "Difficulties are inevitable—that isn't a problem," he says. "I like to go on not only large-scale adventures but also small-scale adventures on one-day rides from my back door. You have to curate your own experience. You have to own every ride."

Leo Rodgers

With one leg and a huge heart,
inspiring people to take chances

Leo Rodgers is used to being stared at. Partly because he's fast and very skilled and prone to doing absurd shit on the bike. And to put it mildly, he doesn't look like your typical expert bike rider—among other distinguishing characteristics, the guy has only one leg.

One night in December 2007, Rodgers had a horrible crash while doing high-speed wheelies on a motorcycle north of his home near Tampa. He fortunately doesn't remember slamming into a guardrail or landing in an alligator-infested river or being resuscitated by medical personnel—he just recalls waking up in a hospital bed with most of his left leg amputated.

But the Leo Rodgers story is not a sad narrative about loss or limitations. It's a story of inspiration and adventure and joy and fearlessness. In 2010, he brushed the cobwebs off his old Redline single-speed, and pretty much everything changed for him after that. When you watch Rodgers ride a bike, the word *disabled* does not come to mind. He has earned eight medals at the U.S. Paralympics Cycling

Open—the national championship for disabled track riders. He has completed very long rides at marquee gravel events like Unbound and Grinduro. He has been filmed on daredevil city rides by urban-riding legend and filmmaker Lucas Brunelle (see page 61).

Around Tampa, he has led all-day gravel adventures and nighttime group rides through neighborhoods that many white riders might not otherwise visit. Whenever he's on a bike, Rodgers is hucking curbs and going quite a bit faster than he should.

"I ride a bike to feel free," says Rodgers, who moved from Tampa to Miami after a stint in Southern California. Rodgers embodies the spirit of adventure because every ride he does—whether it's on a remote mountain trail or a cobbled city street—bristles with the ambition to have fun and push limits and otherwise refuse to be defined by what most people would call a disability. He says he's learned that his purpose in life is to inspire people—to show them that they too can go big and have a blast doing it.

Rodgers crashes a lot. He doesn't crash because he lacks skill; he crashes because he is unafraid to fail. On a rambling ride I did with him around Tampa, we pedaled up a tight triple-decker corkscrew to reach a footbridge over I-275. On the steep, twisty descent, he led the way on a fixed-gear bike without brakes. He had no interest in cautiously backpedaling from the top; instead, he tried to skid down the ramp as fast as he could. About two-thirds of the way down, his rear wheel slid out. Rodgers slammed into the chain-link fencing, sending him over the handlebar and onto the pavement. But even with a minor bruise gestating under his eye, he popped up laughing, jumped back on his bike, and took off. Rodgers says he's spent years learning to fall, ostensibly explaining all his inevitable crashes but perhaps contextualizing his whole approach to life: "A big part of falling is always being mentally prepared to get up."

This no-holds-barred approach to his riding life was once again tested late in 2022, when Rodgers was injured in yet another crash.

The week before Christmas, someone driving an SUV hit Leo in Miami, leaving him with a fractured neck and another long round of rehab. But if anyone knows how to pedal out of a physical challenge, it's Leo Rodgers.

Svein Tuft

An epic adventurer who happens to be a former pro bike racer

The idea that riding can be challenging and exploratory without being competitive is gaining traction within the pro cycling community. The sport is rooted in barnstorming and athletic absurdity, but in recent history, bike racing has been scientific, highly structured, and intensely regulated. Lately, though, lots of pros and recently retired pros have been showing up at big gravel races, clearly enjoying the sense of community and the self-supported philosophy and perhaps the presence of good beer. You see more pros posting about unpaved rambles and bikepacking trips and long adventures that are less about structured training and more about spirited exploration.

No former pro racer embodies this growing sense of adventure better than Svein Tuft. Born in British Columbia, Tuft competed as a pro for fifteen years, winning fourteen Canadian national titles and finishing the Tour de France and Giro d'Italia ten times. He succeeded as a pro because he had a big engine, but he got into riding for the adventure.

Tuft was a rock climber before he was a cyclist, and he started doing long rides as a teenager to get from his home to the top climbing spots in British Columbia. His interest in riding took off from there. Tuft likes to feel like a nomad sometimes. "I've always thought that a life where you carry everything you need on your bike sounds so appealing," he says.

When he was just nineteen, Tuft rode from his home to Alaska. He had a crappy mountain bike and a trailer he had welded, mostly to carry his dog, an 80-pound (27 kg) chow–German shepherd mix named Bear. "It was such a feeling of freedom," Tuft says. "I had no attachments."

Even when he was preparing to compete at the highest level of the sport, Tuft built adventures into his training regime. "I never looked at training like doing the same twenty-five-minute climb," he says. "I need to see some new shit. Adventure has always been the thing. Otherwise, the racing life is a bubble. You're so focused on looking forward that you often miss the moments you're in."

After describing two bikepacking trips in BC, Tuft explains why he loves bike touring so much. He loves how he might start talking to someone random, and an hour later he's having dinner in their home—and then the next day painting their fence to put some cash in his pocket. In short, he loves the way he doesn't know what will happen—that the only way to know what's over the next pass is to go over it. "I find it strange if you don't find this exciting. It's the one thing that gives me childhood glee," he says.

Tuft knows that life can beat you down if you let it. That riding hard is satisfying but not enough to complete his riding life. He admits he doesn't know what he's searching for on these rambles; he only knows that he tends to find it.

Marley Blonsky

Showing the world that all bodies belong on bikes

Marley Blonsky is brave. The Seattle-based rider is passionate about gravel riding and bikepacking—passionate about encouraging others to pursue good times and unknown destinations on a bike. Blonsky is fat. I'm honestly pretty uncomfortable typing that word, but Blonsky uses it herself without any drama. And she was able to leverage her openness about her size to become an ambassador for powerful and progressive bike brands, talking openly in expertly edited videos and Instagram posts about her experiences as an adventure rider who looks different than the typical endurance influencer. She's hardly looking for sympathy; she's looking for good times and new discoveries and a chance to inspire others.

Blonsky says she likes taking wrong turns—going on rides where improvisation is part of the plan. She's also living proof that you don't have to be an elite athlete to have a big adventure. Blonsky says that unlike many of her bike friends, who are into "epic" adventures, she prefers so-called Type 1 fun—trips that are actually fun while they're happening.

Blonsky has ridden the off-road Corvallis to the Sea Trail in Oregon, bikepacked in the Columbia River Gorge, and rambled in the San Juan Islands. "I try to set an intention for each trip," she says. "Maybe I'm feeling grateful, or I want everyone to feel included." She says her favorite trip was an overnight bikepacking adventure near The Dalles, Oregon, with about twenty-five other women. The highlight of that 60-mile (97 km) adventure, she says, was sharing a gorgeous campsite and the experience with a group of like-minded riders.

Though she is totally comfortable riding alone, she often goes on adventures with groups knowing she will be the slowest climber by far. She admits that she sometimes finds this a tough limitation to accept. But then she pivots to the positive—the way it's taught her to do things her own way, at her own pace. "There are no trophies for this," she says. "People just want to test their bodies. It's all about personal satisfaction."

You can find adventure on any kind of ride, but singletrack is often an express lane to a wild time.

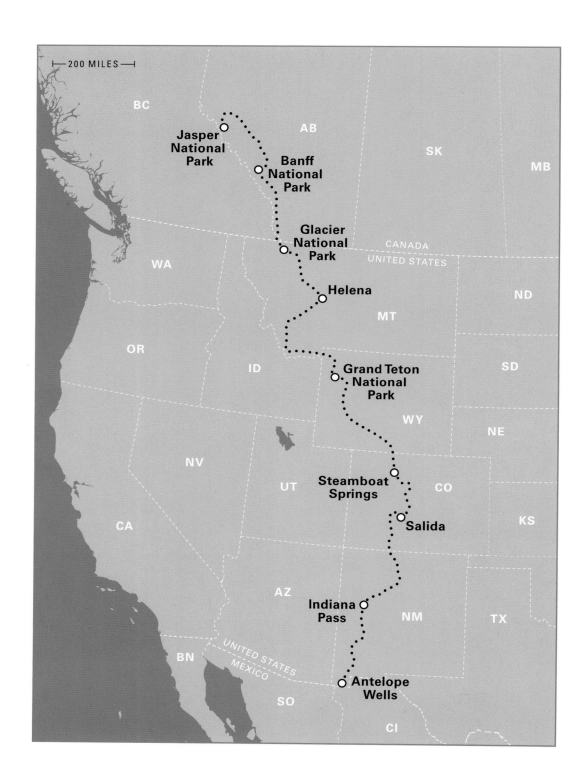

Live to Ride

The Great Divide Mountain Bike Route

The biggest and boldest unpaved adventure in North America

BY THE NUMBERS

· *2,696 miles (4,340 km)*

· *90 percent unpaved*

· *200,000+ feet (60,960+ m) elevation gain*

· *11,910-foot (3,630 m) high point (Indiana Pass in Colorado)*

For those who have the fitness and spirit to tackle one of the toughest off-pavement cycling routes in the world, riding the Great Divide Mountain Bike Route could be a life-changing experience. Running from Banff in Alberta, Canada, to the Mexican border with New Mexico, the GDMBR is not exceptionally technical, but it is very long, with tons of climbing at altitude, and it is at times very remote. Parts of the route pass through grizzly country. But as a reward, riders can traverse the spine of the Rocky Mountains, earning access to a parade of staggering remote beauty that very few riders ever see. The route has become well known for an annual self-supported race, the Tour Divide, but for most of us, traveling with less urgency is the way to go. The route will feel endless at times, but the memories that riders get will fuel the imagination for a lifetime.

- The Canadian portion of the route takes riders through Banff and a series of other national and provincial parks. Riders are encouraged to carry bear spray since much of this remote wilderness area is grizzly territory.

- The journey through Montana and Wyoming begins with days of riding through dense forest and then wide-open valleys. The route skirts the Glacier, Yellowstone, and Grand Teton national parks—meaning riders may see elk and moose and can hit blue-ribbon fishing streams and quiet hot springs.

- The journey across Colorado takes riders through expansive aspen stands and wildflower meadows, historic tourist towns like Steamboat Springs and Breckenridge, and long stretches above the tree line. The crossing of Indiana Pass marks the high point of the whole route.

- The final 600 miles (966 km) go through New Mexico; the climbs get shorter and steeper, water sources get scarcer, and in the small towns along the route, more people speak Spanish than English. Late-summer monsoons can make roads impassable, but the route is also full of geological and anthropological wonders.

Salsa Warbird

The godfather of gravel bikes

Long-distance gravel riding became popular before gravel bikes existed. People often rode cyclocross bikes at gravel races or on long unpaved rambles. These bikes had the right tires for these long adventures but battered their riders. Luckily, a number of people who worked for Salsa Cycles were into the scene, and around 2008 or 2009, the company started developing a new kind of bike. It was called the Warbird, and it had a longer wheelbase, higher clearance (for mud), disc brakes, and a frame oriented for stability

Apidura Frame Pack

*A versatile bag that's
ready for adventure*

Whether you're interested in
big adventures (like a multi-
week bikepacking expedition)
or a more bite-size journey
(like a regular commute), a
durable frame pack is efficient
and convenient, a way to
carry a bunch of gear without
screwing up the handling of a
bike and keep all that essential
stuff—especially snacks and
repair tools—in easy reach.
London-based Apidura's bags
are rugged, lightweight, easy
to install, and waterproof, and
they come in enough sizes
to work with any frame. The
main pocket is big enough to
hold tubes, tools, a pump, and
tons of food, while the external
mesh pocket is perfect for
wrappers and change. This
is the kind of bag that could
give you years of dependable
service even in the nastiest
conditions.

and comfort. The Warbird was
released in 2013, essentially
giving birth to the now
popular gravel bike category.
Like the whole category, the
Warbird has evolved in the
intervening years. Today it
has a carbon fiber frame,

is compatible with multiple
wheel sizes and tires up to 51
millimeters, and comes with
an array of mounts to hold
various bags, racks, fenders,
and water bottles. The bike
that started it all is still
pushing the envelope.

How Bikecentennial led to the birth of bike touring in America

During the summer of 1976, thousands of riders pedaled coast-to-coast as part of Bikecentennial, a groundbreaking event that essentially brought bike touring into the mainstream in the United States.

Sometimes it's hard to pinpoint exactly when a significant cultural inflection point occurred, but in the case of adventure-oriented bike riding in the United States, it's absolutely clear: It all began in the summer of 1976 with a groundbreaking cross-country bike tour called Bikecentennial. As America celebrated its two-hundredth birthday, more than four thousand riders, representing all fifty states and numerous foreign countries, set off to the east or west in small groups in search of adventure. Suddenly, bike touring was on the map.

Dan and Lys Burden remember the night in March 1973 when the whole idea was born. Along with another couple, Greg and June Siple, they were in a small town in Baja California called El Chocolate, in the middle of a massive bike tour from Alaska to Argentina. "Back then, it was so rare to tour," Dan recalls. "You never met another cyclist. No one understood what we were doing." But that night in El Chocolate, the four riders sat around a campfire and talked about the idea of an organized cross-country ride to celebrate the bicentennial.

The original idea was for just an unsupported mass-participation ride from San Francisco to Philadelphia, but soon the four of them started dreaming of something considerably more organized. It was not exactly a stroke of good luck, but a month or two later Dan got severely ill with hepatitis—meaning he and Lys abandoned the Argentina trip and had the bandwidth to throw themselves into planning the Bikecentennial event.

Almost overnight, the kind of riding the Burdens and their friends had done only a few years earlier, as outliers, was a nascent cultural phenomenon.

Lys ran point on creating the route. It took her the better part of a year, as she was looking for historic places and scenic routes wherever possible. She got road maps and placed orange dots on the interesting spots, then looked for blue highways that connected them.

During the summer of 1974, two scouting teams rode two routes Lys had mapped out. Ultimately, they decided on the longer of the two. It was a 4,250-mile (6,840 km) route that connected Astoria, Oregon, to the Yorktown/Williamsburg area in Virginia; crossed the Continental Divide nine times; and passed through national parks like Yellowstone and Grand Teton.

Likely because the idea of such a tangible celebration of the bicentennial was so captivating, support rolled in. Brands like Huffy, *National Geographic*, and Shimano lent financial support to the ride. And big magazines were into it, too. Many publications—twenty or thirty, according to Dan, including *Playboy*, *Sports Illustrated*, and *Parade*—wrote big stories about Bikecentennial. This led to hundreds of inquiries before the ride even began.

In the end, a staggering 4,100 riders participated. A little less than half rode the full route, while the rest did segments from two weeks to halfway. About 1,000 riders participated as "independents"—doing their route solo—and the rest did it in ten- to twelve-person groups with volunteer leaders trained by the Bikecentennial team. Every day for more than a month, one group left each end point going east or west. "The staggered groups meant that tons of people could experience the outdoors without plagues of humans being in one place at the same time," says Lys.

This was nothing like existing bike tours in Europe, where participants stayed in relatively posh hostels with fully stocked kitchens. Bikecentennial riders slept on the floors of school gyms or church halls or in campgrounds. Nearly everyone rode in casual clothing—jeans or gym shorts and T-shirts. The riders ranged in age from teenagers to sixtysomethings, but most were young people who didn't have careers and mortgages.

Dan and Lys spent the summer in Missoula, Montana, where Bikecentennial—rebranded in the 1990s as Adventure Cycling—was based. It was like a war room that ran 24/7.

Almost no one who participated in Bikecentennial wore technical clothing or used ultralight equipment, but the steel bikes of that era were well suited to touring.

With so many inexperienced bike tourers traveling long distances with novice leaders, there was bound to be some chaos. Dan recalls that dozens of people started showing up in Missoula quite sick. "That was kind of crazy—we had to call in the CDC and set up a big tent for these people," he says. "It turned out that some riders had drunk contaminated water at an Idaho campground."

But all the sick riders got better, and exponentially more had what Dan calls a "life-changing experience" participating in Bikecentennial. "Germans have this term and tradition called the Wanderjahr," he says. "It means 'the year of wandering.' This is missing in our culture."

And after 1976, this sort of extended wandering became increasingly popular in the United States. Almost overnight, the kind of riding the Burdens and their friends had done on their own only a few years earlier, as outliers, was a nascent cultural phenomenon. Towns along the routes, which remained in use after 1976, were changed forever by the influx of bike adventurers.

When they look back now, more than four decades after their big ride, the one dreamt up in the Mexican desert, Dan and Lys are proud and amazed to see how bike touring, bikepacking, and other two-wheeled adventures have taken hold today. "When you travel long distances on a bike, you experience things differently, in the way that you meet people and see new things and grow," Dan says. "I like to say that bikes are learning machines."

"When you travel long distances on a bike, you experience things differently," says Dan Burden, articulating a beautiful truth about bike touring.

SPEED

Think back to your earliest days, riding a bicycle as a kid. Chances are, it's a nostalgic exercise. Most passionate bike folks have wonderful memories of childhood riding that stay with them. That feeling of freedom, the way you could explore your neighborhood and then far beyond—that sense of discovery never really goes away for most riders. Likewise for the sense of exciting unpredictability, the way a simple trip so frequently became a grand adventure. The same is true of the thrill of experiencing speed on a bicycle. You carry your earliest flirtations with going fast with you forever.

I grew up in a leafy suburb of New York City that's full of quiet streets and undulating terrain, and I fell in love with the joys of descending. As I got older, I realized that the hills weren't as big as I remembered them to be, but as a child, I found going down those hills enormously exciting. With the wind in my hair and my eyes tearing, I had this palpable feeling of testing the limits of control. I was so enamored with that feeling that I soon began pedaling up those hills so I could tear down them again. These days, I climb to test myself or get fit, but back then, I rode uphill just so I could ride downhill. Maybe you did the same.

I still access these sense memories, and I suspect a lot of bike riders access theirs, too. I have a catalog of greatest hits that I replay all the time: The forty-five-minute scorchers down legit alpine passes—like the rocket-ship ride on a steel bike down East Rim Drive off the plateau of the Grand Canyon or the white-knuckle corkscrew down Monte Grappa in northern Italy on a

You certainly don't have to race or pursue a traditional training program to enjoy the pure joy of riding fast. The simple truth is that fast is fun.

top-of-the-line Pinarello Dogma. Those bucket-list tailwind rides, where spinning 35 mph (56 kph) for an hour was possible, even with panniers on my bike. That morning I piloted a Trek Slash the whole way down California's Mammoth Mountain without grabbing the brakes once. The fastest commute I ever had coming home from work in LA—on a single-speed with deep-section Mavic wheels. The time I rode through a torrential rainstorm at the Tour de Tucson and somehow still had great legs in my fifth hour of riding. These are all memories that make me smile.

Bicycles can do so many different things—they can provide basic transportation and transcendent adventure and physical and mental well-being—but it is undeniable that they also can be instruments of excitement. When I was editor in chief of *Bicycling* magazine, I was pretty cynical about running a cover line like "Fast and Fun," but it always did well on newsstands. And it spoke volumes to what recreational enthusiasts really love about riding bikes: going fast.

There are so many cycling questions that have nothing to do with racing, where speed is the answer. What's the best way to get through a tricky technical section on a mountain bike? What if you're riding to work and are running a few minutes late to a meeting? What if you're cruising through rolling terrain in the countryside and want to put a big smile on your face? Going a bit faster is the answer.

This is not an essay about competition. In my life, I've raced bikes enough to know that I am not particularly good at it but also enough to see how the whole enterprise of racing can trigger an enormous visceral response. There are elements of the sensations and experiences of racing that say more about poetry than performance. Racing can provide a heightened sense of awareness, a flood of adrenaline and other euphoric stuff, and an overload of visual stimulation.

Over a rather prosaic decade of racing bikes, my happiest memories involved sitting in the middle of a huge pack of considerably stronger riders, as completely in the moment as one can be. There were so many bodies and bikes within inches of me, and I was completely shielded from the wind and as fit as I ever will be. It was like being an integral part of a human roller coaster. It was as if the world slowed down as the pack sped up, and there was this intoxicating immersion in going so fast in such a dynamic environment.

But tons of riders chase this euphoric flow state without ever pinning on a number for a race. People who are passionate about mountain biking obviously love to connect with nature, but most of them also love the sensations of speed—whether they are bombing down a steep trail at a ski resort or railing banked turns on a purpose-built trail or simply flowing down technical singletrack through a blur of greenery. Like so many other kinds of bikes, mountain bikes can be a bit wobbly or balky at slow speeds and get more stable and capable as they go faster. Anyone who has pedaled through rocks and roots and sand knows that

Bicycles can do so many different things—
they can provide basic transportation and
transcendent adventure and physical and
mental well-being—but it is undeniable that
they also can be instruments of excitement.

picking up speed almost always makes these obstacles easier to navigate. Well-designed mountain bikes always want to go a little faster.

The folks who like to wander on road bikes have their own love affair with speed. Even at moderate speeds, pedaling a bicycle on rolling terrain is work—it can range from invigorating effort to existential toil—and cruising downhill is almost always glorious payback. There is something undeniably delicious about coasting down a hill that you surmounted under your own power. The bicycle allows you to recover as you are treated to a theme-park-quality experience. I have been on many group rides in such a moment, and if I have the presence of mind to look around at my companions, I often notice that everyone is smiling. It's that childhood sense memory coming back in full glory.

You don't have to fly downhill to feel it. You can be with a small group of friends, riding faster and with less effort than you possibly could alone. You can receive that gift when you're lucky enough to have the wind at your back, when small shifts in hyperlocal weather can bring joy and sorrow. You can get that feeling when you do fifteen hard pedal strokes to get through a traffic signal before the light turns red, that tiny burst of euphoria that comes from knowing your body can respond when called upon.

Thankfully, the bike industry is full of good engineers, framebuilders, and product managers who enable all this fun. It's easy to criticize the biggest companies that make and sell bikes—for catering to the high-end consumer; for making racier bikes than most folks need; for making too many black, white, and red frames—but the reality remains that the quality of nearly every bike in your neighborhood bike shop is very high. Within a few years, the technology and designs that debuted at the Tour de France have trickled down to bikes that cost a fraction of those rarefied thoroughbreds. The pace of such improvement has gotten so fast that even entry-level bikes from second-tier brands can be counted on to deliver a surprising amount of spirited performance. They are designed to be fast and fun.

Specialized, one of the two giants of the industry (Trek being the other), has made a decade-long bet on the marketing campaign "Aero Is Everything." Like any catchy marketing slogan, it's a bit

The fabled gravel roads of Tuscany may not be the easiest to rip, but there's a thrill to finding your technical limit.

ridiculous—because comfort and weight and reliability and other things are still something—but I admire the way Specialized has chased and disseminated this point of view. Chris D'Aluisio, a longtime development guru at the company, is an articulate advocate for how incremental improvements to aerodynamics and stiffness do more than help pros (and recreational racers) win bike races—they allow the rest of us to ride a little bit faster without making all the sacrifices demanded of elite athletes. "What I notice by working with the best riders is that their observations always translate to the average rider," he says. "We all go through the same air, and we all generally want to go farther and faster with less energy."

And while the most obvious applications of these observations relate to enthusiasts chasing fitness and performance, they also apply to the least sporty corners of the bike world. Nearly every sort of ride is a little bit more fun if you can go a little bit faster. This is true on rail trails and gravel roads and urban bike lanes. Anybody who has ever ridden anywhere with a kid knows this is true: Each ride can be a lively escapade.

I log thousands of miles every year on the beachfront bike paths of Los Angeles County and see folks on stately cruisers and big-box-bought hybrids—I see them extending their feet off the pedals when they coast downhill and rocking their shoulders with pleasurable labor to get a little extra speed in a tailwind. And likewise, I've seen thousands of bike-share users in big cities like New York and Washington, DC, pursue the inconsequential glory of a speedy-ish commute, the way a trip borne of utility and purpose sparked some moments of playful effort. Even a heavy city bike likes to go a bit faster if you're up for it.

E-bikes are changing the game, too, in the way they let people commute to work or run errands or otherwise replace car trips. E-bikes will revolutionize urban transport and have the potential to be a vital climate-action tool. They are staggeringly efficient machines.

But they also are a shitload of fun to ride. Many people have never experienced the feeling of getting a well-engineered bicycle up to speed—and many others haven't done it in decades or associate it with suffering they don't find appealing. E-bikes can be a gateway drug to the addictive, exuberant sensations of riding a bicycle. It's really a glorious privilege if you are a committed road cyclist who, thanks to the right mix of training and equipment and experience, can regularly pass through the world at 17 miles (27 km) per hour or faster, but there's really no downside to expanding that thrill to other demographics, as long as they do it safely.

For years, I have been watching with interest as different government entities try to regulate the speed of e-bikes. It's impossible to make everyone happy, balancing utility, performance, safety, and manufacturing standards. In my opinion, the Class 3 e-bikes allowed in much of the United States, which can hit 28 mph (45 kph) before the motor cuts off, go a bit too fast for many users, encouraging relatively inexperienced riders to hit bike-racing

The fearsome Stelvio in the Italian Alps, one of the most photographed climbs in the world, is also a thrilling challenge to descend.

> Riding is addictively fun, and the fitter you get, the more narcotic it becomes. You can ride a little faster without suffering, it feels like play rather than work, and you often step off the bike feeling more refreshed than exhausted.

speeds in complicated and pedestrian-heavy urban and suburban areas. And the EU standards, capping most e-bikes at 16 mph (26 kph), are just a little bit slow—in the United States, at least. That's why I love the Class 1 and 2 e-bikes available in the United States—riding 20 mph (32 kph) is at once thrilling, efficient, and safe in most (but not all) settings. Having the bikes seem legitimately fun will help them change the world.

Whatever kind of bike you choose, riding a bit more and improving your fitness will yield so many positive benefits. You will feel healthier and more confident. You will wander farther and see more of your community. You will likely sleep better and feel more whole and more focused in your work.

But it's even better than all that. You'll have more fun, too. This is something that people who don't ride struggle to understand, especially if they also spend a ton of time in a car stuck in traffic. Riding is addictively fun, and the fitter you get, the more narcotic it becomes. You can ride a little faster without suffering, it feels like play rather than work, and you often step off the bike feeling more refreshed than exhausted. This is why so many riders chase fitness and plot to get a lighter or more spirited bike—not because they want to win a race or set a Strava PR or beat their friends to a town line sign. They do it because it just feels so good.

One of the more cinematic examples of this phenomenon was an event called the LA Marathon Crash Race, which later became the LA Marathon Crash Ride. It's now defunct—arguably a victim of its own viral success. It was one of the most strangely wonderful rides I've ever done. It was the furthest thing from a normal race or even a normal ride. You don't usually meet for a ride outside a Vietnamese donut shop at 3:30 a.m. But that's exactly where I and a couple thousand other riders were—on Sunset Boulevard in Hollywood, near Tang's Donuts (sadly closed now), waiting for the Crash Ride to begin.

Riding the famed boulevards of Los Angeles is typically defined and confined by the ever-present traffic. Millions of people in cars clog things up and force bike riders to tentatively navigate through the margins. But for a decade, there was one brief window where these fabled streets belonged to bike culture—in the early-morning hours of one day in February or March, after

There are aspects of racing that aren't exactly fun, but the sensations and all-consuming demands of riding in a fast-moving group can be narcotic.

the Los Angeles Marathon course had been barricaded but before the starting gun sounded.

The Crash Race started as a renegade free-for-all, mushroomed into a semi-regulated phenomenon, and then collapsed under its own weight. No one ever paid a cent to participate or signed a waiver. The participants represented the full spectrum of LA bike culture—the road racers and the fixie kids, people of every race and ethnicity, folks on every manner of bike, some riders looking to race and others looking to test themselves and others just looking for a predawn parade.

When I did it in 2015, the event was already dying. The police presence was strong, meant to discourage the no-holds-barred racing that had defined the event in the past and made the city's lawyers understandably nervous about liability. So it had by then become a massive fast-paced group ride from Hollywood to the ocean in Santa Monica.

Even in this watered-down form, it was pretty wild. I saw some spectacular crashes; I heard the sound of carbon fiber fracturing; I smelled the aroma of burning rubber as riders on fixed-gear bikes without brakes slid through high-speed corners. It was a parade of reckless joy. The wide streets of car-obsessed cities were ours for sixty minutes, and we lustily flew down Rodeo Drive and Santa Monica Boulevard and San Vicente Boulevard. People hooted and hollered. The point wasn't to win something; the point was to experience this communal and intoxicating rally. The lead pack reached Santa Monica right before the sun came up—the ocean was starting to glimmer—and then wave after wave of riders barreled to the finish. Strangers high-fived each other. It was like we'd been given an hour to be kids again.

The magazine cover line should have said "Fast Is Fun." It's the truth.

Speed is relative. Fondo participants test their fitness by cruising up the Pordoi Pass in the Dolomites as fast as possible.

Lucas Brunelle

Unapologetically Fast and Polarizing

Filmmaker Lucas Brunelle has now spent a couple of decades documenting urban and messenger riding culture in a manner that is easy to argue about and hard to stop watching. "Speed is a way of life for me," he says.

Brunelle's videos show messenger types competing in unsanctioned high-speed races on intensely busy city streets, folks riding on highways or holding on to moving vehicles, and people otherwise riding with what I'd call aggressive poetry. In a variety of truly hairy situations, Brunelle is in the mix, wearing a custom helmet outfitted with a variety of cameras, giving viewers a visceral feeling of what it's like to recklessly fly through an infinitely chaotic urban landscape.

Line of Sight (2012) is my favorite of his films; it includes footage from China, Central America, London, and Mexico City and is anchored by an extended black-and-white montage of street racing in New York. These scenes are the furthest thing from a tutorial on law-abiding riding behavior. Brunelle shadows a few of the very best bike messengers in the world as they disregard just about every law governing cycling other than the laws of physics. The racers fly down one-way streets the wrong way and cruise through red lights and weave through traffic with nausea-inducing grace. I would never ride through New York or London like that, but dismissing the culture or artful attempts to document it is too easy. Bicycles are many things, and a tool of rebellion is one of them. Consider the role bicycles had in the women's empowerment movement in the late nineteenth century or how bikes were such powerful tools and symbols during the social justice movement in the early 2020s.

Brunelle has been at this rebellion thing for a long time. He grew up on Martha's Vineyard and says that his dad and grandmother were daredevil drivers who never paid much attention to speed limits. That made an impression on him. Brunelle got passionate about riding BMX when he was a teenager. "I was getting into a lot of trouble back then," he recalls. He is not exaggerating. There was a trip to reform school and a stint at a psychiatric institution, and there were more than a few run-ins with the police. "Other kids were being pressured not to hang

out with me. Rules were being imposed on me, and I did not exactly like it. The bike was a way to be free, to get away from adults."

Eventually, Brunelle got into road racing and found immediate success. He won races and quickly upgraded to Category 2, which meant he could compete with professional bike racers. He was invited to train at the Olympic & Paralympic Training Center. He enrolled at the University of Massachusetts at Amherst and raced there, too. But already, Brunelle—who is in his fifties and says he still does two or three sanctioned bike races a year—had a sense that bike-racing culture was not a perfect fit for him.

Ultimately, he found the community and excitement he sought in the bike messenger community. He started doing unsanctioned alley cat races—urban events with multiple checkpoints and few rules—and huge critical-mass rides. Brunelle started filming some of these rides and had to go through an intense learning curve. His first success was *Drag Race*, a 2003 short film that chronicled male cyclists dressed in women's clothes racing around New York City.

Over the subsequent twenty years, Brunelle has been a controversial figure within bike culture—for participating in and celebrating high-speed, seemingly risky riding. And he has typically leaned in to this rebel role, making zero apologies while defending the admittedly madcap nature of the riding. "There's no better feeling than speeding down the road," he says. "And it's safer because I'm the center of attention. I feel most at risk when I'm going slow and someone is coming up behind me." Brunelle is the kind of guy who has a few mottoes. One of his favorites is "Ride fast, die last."

But it's more than just bluster for Brunelle. He truly feels most alive when he's on crowded city streets, holding on to the side of a city bus or racing 30 mph (48 kph) among a multitude of cars. "I feel like the earth moves more slowly when I'm going fast," he says. "Cities can be oppressively restrictive and homogenous. Riding fast is vengeance for me. It's a big middle finger. Following the rules is not how I'm going to live. It's rebellion."

Coryn Labecki

*The fastest, most versatile female bike
racer in the US is all about speed*

Over the past two decades, Coryn Labecki
(née Rivera) has won a staggering seventy-two
national championships in four different cycling
disciplines: road racing, mountain biking,
track racing, and cyclocross. Although she has
finessed her way to some big victories, the
diminutive rider typically wins by outsprinting
all comers in a drag race to the finish line.

Labecki says she just loves speed. She
loves to watch Formula 1, she loves to bomb
down a mountain on a snowboard, and she's
been known to twist the throttle on a dirt bike.
"I suppose I'm a speed junkie," Labecki says.
"I like pushing to the edge of the line. And
sometimes I have to experience crossing the
line to know where the limit is."

In many of the interviews Labecki does,
her size becomes part of the conversation.

She is five foot one, weighs about 105 pounds,
and rides an XXS bike. But even though most
world-class sprinters are considerably bigger,
Labecki can bring the heat in a field sprint.
She doesn't know why, exactly. Maybe she has
aerodynamic advantages. Perhaps it's just a
superior power-to-weight ratio. She says she
feels her size helps her corner better than many
competitors and allows her to fit through gaps
other racers couldn't contemplate.

In any case, Labecki has spent the past
fifteen-plus years throwing her hands up in
victory salutes. She says her most meaningful
win was the RideLondon Classique in 2017.
The conditions were far from ideal for a small
rider—the finale was in pouring rain with a
long, flat finishing straight with a tailwind.
But she gritted it out and outsprinted a world-
class field for the win.

Even now, after twenty years of racing,
Labecki says the thrill of the speed remains
a visceral part of racing.

Labecki is well acquainted with the risks of
her trade. If you sprint for big wins in European
pro races or domestic criteriums with a decent
purse, there will be crashes. Once, in Qatar, she
crashed so badly that she woke up in a hospital
bed with no contact lenses in her eyes and no
memory of what had happened.

But still, she is not intimidated by the risks.
Far from it. "When I sprint, it's like everything
is going in slow motion," she says. "It becomes
normal. It's like a zen state. I'm not afraid of the
speed and the consequences. I am aware that
it's crazy dangerous, but I am at ease with the
risks."

How does she remain at ease when she's
sprinting 37 mph (60 kph) while bumping
shoulders with a bunch of hungry competitors?
"Speed to me is about staying in control," she
says. "If you are out of control, then you're not
going as fast as you can."

Chris Holmes

*A bike designer who knows that
every bike likes to go fast*

He's not famous. He's not an elite athlete. He's a product development guy in the bicycle industry, but not the kind of guy who designs race bikes for pro athletes. And yet as someone who has designed and marketed bikes for people who don't race, Chris Holmes knows a lot about speed. He knows that the sense of speed is pivotal to the feeling that riding is a good time.

These days, Holmes is the brand director at Marin, a company that makes fun bikes for people who like to ramble and rumble. Before that, he helped design bikes at Electra, a brand that helped transform cruisers and city bikes. And he's worked at Pacific Cycle, the parent company behind Schwinn, GT, and Mongoose. He's been working on bikes since the mid-1990s.

Like many riders, Holmes traces his passion for riding back to childhood. He grew up in central Illinois and still carries the feeling of freedom of being allowed to stay out on his bike until the streetlights came on. He remembers the two sizable hills in his hometown and the feeling of bombing down them over and over

again. Riding fast is like flying on the ground, Holmes says.

According to Holmes, every bike has a "sweet spot"—a certain speed at which it really comes alive. And he knows that any well-designed bike, whether it's designed to cruise at the beach or transport a kid to school or enable a bikepacking adventure, is made to feel comfortable at speed. Anyone who has ever wobbled around a parking lot at very slow speed on a bike and then experienced how the bike became more stable as they picked up speed knows this firsthand. Holmes says that this stability is due to the gyroscopic effect of the wheels, adding that the design and geometry of a bike frame determine at what speed riders are in that sweet spot. "Within design parameters, bikes just like to go fast," he says.

Greg LeMond

The greatest American bike racer of all time

This is not a narrative synopsis of the most acclaimed American bike racer of the past century. There are books that cover this topic. Wikipedia has a pretty solid summary. No, this is simply a brief introduction to Greg LeMond, three-time Tour de France champion and two-time world champion, and his relationship to speed—how it fit or shaped his personality, how it impacts his approach to designing bicycles, how it makes riding more fun.

LeMond grew up near Carson City, Nevada, and he knows now that his childhood was framed by ADHD. He had trouble sitting still, trouble behaving the way grown-ups wanted him to, and he discovered pretty early on that riding a bike helped center him. By the time he was fourteen, he was regularly heading out for long alpine loops to Lake Tahoe, climbing Spooner Summit and then eventually bombing down from Mount Rose to Reno. "I always liked to climb a lot because it let me go downhill more," he says. "It made me feel alive and alert."

My conversation with LeMond took place in April 2022, roughly six weeks before he made public his diagnosis with leukemia. But the legendary bike racer is no stranger to existential adversity; in 1987, after all, he nearly died in a hunting accident—and came back to win the Tour de France. Roughly a year after his diagnosis, LeMond reported that he was responding well to his treatment and feeling optimistic about his prospects.

For as long as he can recall, LeMond has had a scientific mind, and the release he got from riding fast was more neurochemical than emotional. He says that speed releases dopamine and norepinephrine and serotonin. "It's a powerful feeling, very stimulating."

He loved everything about racing. The way he had to remain hyperfocused while racing in a large, fluid, fast-moving pack. He loved the endless visual stimulation of the world flying by. He loved the physical release of the effort. Racing helped him learn a lot about his body and brain, LeMond says.

Since before his retirement as a pro racer in 1994, LeMond has designed and manufactured bikes in a few business ventures. Talking to him about bicycles is more like spitballing with an engineer than chatting with a marketing executive. He cares about the details—the tensile strength of different carbon fiber composites, the stack and reach and angles of a frame, the length of the crank arms.

LeMond says there's a connection between the qualities of a high-performing bike and the neurochemical joys of riding at speed. That using a lighter, better bike increases the dopamine rush—as does getting fitter. "It's just a beautiful vicious circle," he says, briefly sidetracking into an explanation of why the rotational inertia of good wheels makes riding more satisfying. "You just keep wanting to get fitter and get better bikes and go faster, and you keep getting positive stimuli that what you're doing is working."

These days, LeMond is riding on the road a few days a week for an hour or so. He's dealing with arthritis in his hips complicated by lead poisoning from the 1987 shooting accident. But he's riding, proselytizing for, and most recently developing e-bikes. "E-bikes let people who would never ride a bike because it's too painful get started. It brings more people into the activity," he says. "I ride one all the time. I like to go 28 mph everywhere! Again, there's that visual stimulation. It feels like I'm doing the Tour de France."

Bike riders know that the right road can deliver all of the visceral pleasures of a roller coaster.

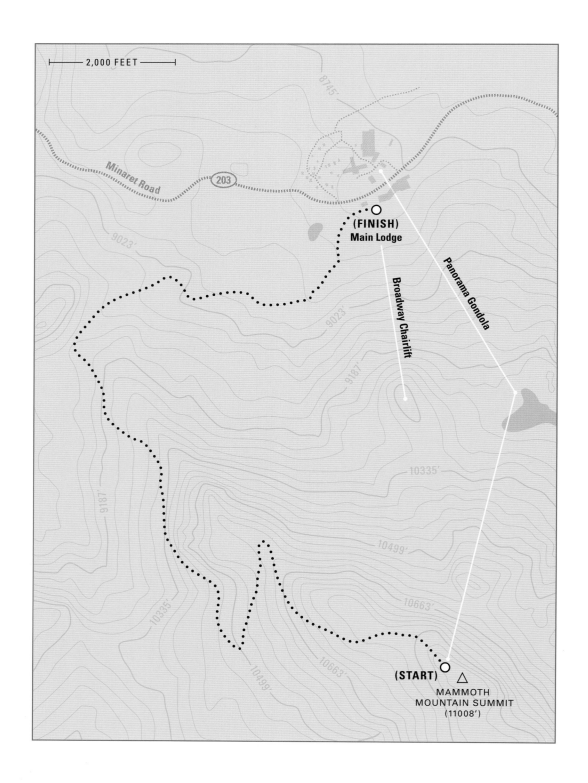

2,000 FEET

8745'

Minaret Road

203

9023'

(FINISH)
Main Lodge

9023'

Panorama Gondola

Broadway Chairlift

9187'

9187'

10335'

10335'

10499'

10663'

10499'

10663'

(START)

MAMMOTH
MOUNTAIN SUMMIT
(11008')

Kamikaze Mountain Bike Trail

The downhill mountain bike course that began a revolution

BY THE NUMBERS

- 3.6 miles (5.8 km)

- 2,100 feet (640 m) elevation change

- Average grade: 12 percent

- Steepest grade: 20 percent

Downhill mountain biking has certainly evolved over the past forty years. Today, top pros descend highly technical courses that integrate rock gardens, steep singletrack, jumps and drops, and other obstacles. An average speed of 25 to 30 mph (40 to 48 kph) is typical. But back in the mid-1980s and the '90s, downhill courses were much less technical and thus much faster. No downhill course from this era is more legendary or faster than the Kamikaze trail at Mammoth Mountain in California. And while today's downhill racers compete with sophisticated and specialized bikes with dual suspension, racers back in the day tackled Kamikaze on bikes that had rudimentary suspension forks or were completely rigid. Still, top racers were regularly surpassing 60 mph (92 kph) on the wide, steep fire roads. Legendary riders from the early days of mountain biking—like John Tomac and Missy Giove—triumphed on Kamikaze, but any enthusiast who buys a lift ticket at Mammoth can take their own stab at glory.

- The course begins at the 11,053-foot (3,369 m) summit of Mammoth Mountain with views of the dramatic spires of the Minarets peaks to the west.

- The course offers up only two tight turns—a left at 0.75 mile (1.2 km) and then a right about 1 mile (1.6 km) from the top.

- 1.8 miles (2.9 km) from the start, the course hits a 20 percent gradient, where a skilled and fearless rider can surpass 60 mph (92 kph).

- 2.25 miles (3.5 km) from the top, the dirt road arcs right. The steepest terrain is now behind riders.

- Roughly 2.75 miles (4.4 km) from the summit, the course veers right onto a trail that traverses a ridge. Riders must pedal pretty hard if they want to retain their speed.

- The course ends near the Broadway Express chairlift, 3.6 miles (5.8 km) from the top. Fast enthusiasts can ride the course in five or six minutes, but pros have broken four minutes.

Scott Gambler 900

Designed and built to go downhill with abandon

There are tons of mountain bikes that can descend trails with aplomb, but for pure speed on steep and technical terrain, nothing can match a really well-designed downhill mountain bike. And in that category, this latest high-end iteration of Scott Gambler's long-successful eponymous line is virtually impossible to beat. With a full carbon frame, it weighs less than 35 pounds (16 kg), which is extremely light for this category, but it has that solid, neutral handling of the very best downhill bikes. Every element of the bike—the geometry, the specs, the suspension system—has been fine-tuned to maximize raw speed on the mountain. If you are not a pro rider, you will hit your own limits before you approach the limits of this bike on gnarly terrain.

Benno RemiDemi

A stylish e-bike that looks and feels fast

All electric bikes sold legally have a government-mandated top speed—in the United States, that's 20 mph (32 kph) for a Class 1 or Class 2 e-bike and 28 mph (45 kph) for a Class 3 e-bike—so the subjective feeling of speed comes from qualitative details. E-bikes that feel fast are invariably spirited, highly maneuverable, and, above all, fun. That's why the Class 1 RemiDemi feels like a speedster; with small wheels, a short wheelbase, wide, slick tires, and a motor from Bosch's Performance Line, the bike is nimble and spunky. And with a clean, playful design, it even looks peppy. Still, it's set up to carry a passenger or tons of cargo—maybe a big grocery shop or a surfboard—so think of it like a small turbocharged station wagon.

Look T20

An iconic track bike for those seeking time-trialing glory

No bike company has captured more Olympic medals than Look—winning gold fourteen times since 1996. And this aero masterpiece, designed for the French track squad for the Tokyo Games, oozes speed and style. The colorway, inspired by Piet Mondrian's paintings, adds class to what otherwise is a purpose-driven beast. Made entirely in France, the bike is lighter, stiffer, and more aerodynamic than its predecessor. Look says that the one-piece crank set is up to 200 percent stiffer than any other crank set. Every detail of the bike—the obsessively mindful carbon fiber weaving, the new rear-wheel thru axle, a seatpost that's adjustable in length and angle—reflects the limitless pursuit of performance.

In the run-up to the Paris Games, Look released a follow-up, the predictably

Enve SES 7.8 Wheels

*High-end wheels that come
to life at high speeds*

If you're riding a triathlon or
time trial, you won't find a faster
or more aerodynamic wheelset.
Handmade in Utah, these
carbon fiber wheels have an
asymmetrical design—the rear
wheel is deeper and narrower
than the front wheel. They're
not the lightest or deepest
premium wheels on the market,
and they're hardly optimal for
a casual ride in crosswinds,
but if you're cranking 25 mph
(40 kph) or more, the 7.8s are
like magic—incredibly fast,
stable, and smooth. For a
classic pairing, get them with
the superbly engineered and
utterly bombproof Chris King
R45 hubs.

Giro Spherical Helmet

*Cutting-edge protection
from high-speed crashes*

Bike helmets are not the answer
to many safety problems
cyclists face, but certainly
for riders who pursue speed,
they are essential. And while
government standards sadly
haven't been updated in years,
consumers can seek out tech-
heavy helmets that integrate
new subsystems to reduce the
odds of a concussion or other
serious brain injuries. This
high-end racing and adventure
helmet contains a new ball-
and-socket design, with inner
and outer liners that can move
independently to redirect
impact forces away from the
brain. It also integrates proven
MIPS (multidirectional impact
protection system) technology
to address the rotational forces
that can cause concussions in
certain crashes. And speed
demons will appreciate the
outstanding ventilation of the
helmet, which has fifteen vents
and channels to help folks stay
cool while they're going hard.

named P24, which features a
wildly futuristic frame design
with a radical two-pronged
seatpost and an unusually
wide fork (both in the name of
aerodynamics). If you have to
ask whether you can afford a
T20 or P24, the answer almost
certainly is no.

How five women transformed bike racing—in the 1890s

In the 1890s, track racers such as Dottie Farnsworth (*above*) and Lizzie Glaw barnstormed across the country to great acclaim, challenging many people's perceptions about the toughness of women.

For a decade or two, bicycle racing was perhaps the biggest sport in America. Starting in the 1880s, when the so-called safety bicycle began to replace the penny-farthing, bicycle riding (and racing) became an enormous fad. This movement impacted many groups in the United States. Numerous books and movies have documented the amazing story of Marshall "Major" Taylor, a Black bike racer who dominated track sprinting right before and after the turn of the century and was one of the most celebrated athletes of his time. Comparatively little attention has been given to a handful of women who came before him as pioneering bike racers, the riders who will forever be known as the Big Five.

Their names—May Allen, Tillie Anderson, Helen Baldwin, Dottie Farnsworth, and Lizzie Glaw—are all worth googling. In 1895, promoters in the Northeast and Midwest began staging races just for women. One promotor held races on small wooden tracks, known widely as velodromes, and allowed the women to compete in tights rather than bloomers. These races were an immediate sensation—because of both the quality of the racing, which somehow surprised the public, and the provocative outfits the riders wore. Thousands of spectators turned out every night for these exhibitions.

The Big Five barnstormed across the middle of the country for the rest of the 1890s, delighting crowds and challenging people's preconceptions about the toughness and endurance of women. Tillie Anderson—who earned the awesome nickname "Tillie the

Helen Baldwin (*left*) and Lizzie Glaw thrilled large crowds for more than a decade, changing public perceptions of how women were capable of racing at the highest level.

The Big Five barnstormed across the middle of the country for the rest of the 1890s, delighting crowds and challenging people's preconceptions about the toughness and endurance of women.

Terrible Swede"—was undoubtedly the dominant rider of the group, winning something like 123 of the 130 races she entered (Glaw was the only one to beat her more than once). Anderson had previously made a living working as a seamstress and spent the better part of a year saving to buy her first bike. Then she began training relentlessly. While most of her competitors were feted for being pretty, Anderson (and Lizzie Glaw) took some crap for looking too masculine or plain. In a way that remains an issue 130 years later, simply being a world-class athlete wasn't enough for many fans.

But all five women became well-paid celebrity athletes. Six-day races were arguably the first mass-spectator arena events in the United States, and these women were stars. They raced in Madison Square Garden and other famous venues of the era.

But unlike Major Taylor and other men who raced on the track, and who rode into even greater fame over the next decade, the Big Five faded into obscurity when the entire women's bicycle racing scene collapsed in 1902. Farnsworth, who had a side gig riding with a touring circus, collapsed on a track and died soon thereafter due to a blood infection that had no apparent connection to her riding. Nonetheless, the League of American Wheelmen promptly banned women from riding in six-day races, a prohibition that lasted until 1958.

Still, the Big Five's impact was felt worldwide. In 1896, Susan B. Anthony wrote an oft-cited passage about how bikes were empowering women: "I think [the bicycle] has done more to emancipate women than any one thing in the world. I rejoice every time I see a woman ride by on a bike. It gives her a feeling of self-reliance and independence the moment she takes her seat; and away she goes, the picture of untrammeled womanhood."

The Big Five were far ahead of their time. They were riding to proclaim their independence in the most provocative fashion, destroying their culture's preconceptions about how women could lead their lives and perform as athletes and even dress in public. Their determination to race, to feel the joys of speed and competition, remains an inspiration today.

Tillie Anderson was the dominant racer of the era. The former seamstress, who won more than 90 percent of the races she entered, was posthumously inducted into the U.S. Bicycling Hall of Fame in 2000.

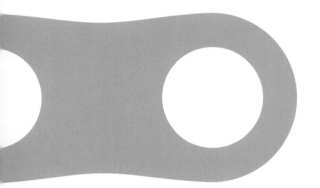

UTILITY

It is after midnight in Los Angeles. The side streets are empty, and the big boulevards are oddly desolate, too. It's quiet enough for me to hear the generators of the taco trucks humming as I pedal past, inhaling the aroma of roasting carnitas. I'm on a road bike with a messenger bag slung over my back and an LED headlight throwing a cone of illumination onto the pavement, cruising home after a long day of work. I'm thinking about the feature I just edited, fantasizing about what I'm going to eat when I get home, and keeping an eye out for incompetent drivers, but mostly I'm just lost in an endless rumination. The commute is many things, but above all, it is time to unplug from the rest of my life.

Before I moved to Los Angeles in 2014, I had a radically different riding life. I was, in retrospect, an enthusiast. This doesn't mean I didn't experience or understand the existential qualities of riding a bike, but the truth is that I had spent about fifteen years pursuing fun and fitness, competition and community, adventure, and restorative suffering. These are all beautiful things, and they were so engaging that I did not once contemplate whether I could have a rich riding life without or beyond them.

But moving to LA changed everything. My wife and I wound up renting a house near the beach that was nowhere near the Mid-City office of the *Hollywood Reporter*, where I would be working. I had sold my car before I left Pennsylvania and was far from eager to buy another one to battle LA's infamous traffic twice a day. I had a new, time-consuming job; a home in a densely populated metropolis; a substantial commute; and two kids in elementary school—in other words, my life was not conducive to undertaking the kind of daily recreational training I'd been doing for years. And it was late summer, a time of year in coastal Southern California when the weather is endlessly perfect—not hot, not cold, not rainy, yet somehow not monotonous. So I decided to start riding a bike to and from work every day.

That decision transformed my life. In the next six years, I rode more than 40,000 miles (64,000 km) just going back and forth between my house and my offices in Mid-City and then Santa Monica. For a couple of years, I continued to roll out for weekend adventures—joining competitive group rides or training to do long, hilly endurance events—but ultimately, I realized that my bike commuting was hard and engaging enough that I could completely dedicate my weekends to my family and my writing and my recovery. My commuting became my whole riding life.

For the first time since I was an adolescent, when I depended on my maroon Fuji ten-speed to transport myself to school and friends' houses and stores in my suburban hometown, I was riding primarily for utility. I was using my bike not as a fitness implement or a sophisticated plaything for exploration, but as a tool to get me where I needed to go, to do all the things I had relied on a car to do for so many years. And in a manner I didn't foresee, I was blown away by the utility of the bicycle.

I was hardly the first or the only one to make such a discovery. Over the fifteen years preceding the Covid-19 pandemic, which brought its own seismic shifts, American participation in bike riding was mostly flat. Likewise, the number of people participating in things like bike races and charity rides or buying high-performance equipment was pretty stagnant. But meanwhile, riding in American cities exploded. Millions of people discovered that getting around on a bike is more efficient, pleasant, inexpensive, healthy, and sustainable than using a car in some situations.

This revolution is still in its early days, but already, the changes—the way bike culture has evolved and the way the broader culture is shifting—are transformative. For a long time, American riders have regarded with envy the utility riding culture in Europe. Cities like Copenhagen and Amsterdam and Oslo, thoroughly redesigned in the 1970s (and beyond) to be perfect for riding around town, have led the way. These are places where everyone seems to be on a bike, where riders are the VIPs and drivers are the guests. But change has also come to many of the biggest cities in Europe—sprawling urban centers like London and Berlin and Barcelona and especially Paris—which are embracing micromobility and community and taking deliberate action with climate change in mind. North American cyclists are watching the transformation of these once car-centric cities with hope about what could happen if their civic leaders and planning institutions really got behind making their cities safer and better for riding.

E-bikes have had a revolutionary impact on how people get around—allowing people to go farther and carry more with a big grin on their face.

But even though the pace at home is slower than many North American riders wish it were, the reality is that the metamorphosis has begun. In the past decade, North American cities have built thousands of miles of bike lanes to accommodate and attract riders. This process is very far from perfect, facing all sorts of resistance and apathy from the public and powerful institutions, but it nonetheless has changed the game. In so-called bike-friendly communities, the number of people who get around town on a bike has mushroomed.

To appreciate the scale of this growth in utility riding, ponder the success story that is Citi Bike in New York City. This bike-share program, launched on Memorial Day weekend in 2013, has redefined transportation in the largest US city. The bikes were at first available only in Manhattan south of 59th Street and in a few Brooklyn neighborhoods. Initially, critics mocked the idea, moaning loudly that the docking stations were an ugly waste of space and predicting an epic failure. But then New Yorkers and visitors fell in love with Citi Bike. In 2019, the last full year before the pandemic, users went on 21 million rides and pedaled more than 36.5 million miles (58.7 million km) on the now-iconic blue bikes. Stations spread throughout Manhattan and Brooklyn, with many also added in Queens and the Bronx and even cities in New Jersey. And after Covid altered the region's access to public transit and indoor exercise, the popularity of Citi Bike grew even more. In July and August 2022, users rode more than 12 million miles (19 million km) around New York. That's like riding to the moon and back twenty-five times!

But this renewed interest in biking extends beyond New York and bike-share programs. Big cities like Chicago, Washington, Minneapolis, and San Francisco have seen way more riders and bike lanes, and tons of smaller cities have jumped on the bandwagon, too. Especially where cities have built infrastructure that makes newer riders feel safe, there have been seismic shifts in the demographics of people riding, with increased participation from women, people of color, and senior riders. The streets belong to everyone.

There have been utility riders in North America for decades—die-hard commuters who pedal through rain and snow to get to work, "pro" cyclists like bike messengers and delivery riders, and folks who like to take a leisurely spin to their neighborhood coffee shop or café. But nothing that matches the scale of what we're seeing now. You can go to boutique clothing stores or high-end markets and see stylish casual bikes mounted on the walls or window displays to highlight the shift in public consciousness about transit riding—riding these bikes is often now emblematic of the good life. You can go to hip neighborhoods in so many US cities and see corrals full of locked bikes that people rode to go shopping or to lunch or happy hour. Utility riding is no longer just for the fit or the brave.

The relatively recent popularity of electric bikes has helped accelerate this welcome change, too. Though there remains some

Bike messengers have led the way when it comes to how to approach and equip oneself for city riding.

confusion and skepticism about e-bikes from both within and outside of bike culture, they are most certainly bicycles and most certainly a positive development. In sprawling, hilly, and warm-weather cities, they exponentially increase the number of people who can realistically replace car trips with a bike ride, and they create a new group of stakeholders who can amplify the demand for safer places to ride. I bought an electric cargo bike in 2017, and frankly, it radically improved my transit riding. Because the bike is outfitted with two huge panniers, I can use it to do a big family shop at the grocery store—with zero inconvenience. Now I don't have to battle the parking chaos at Whole Foods or Trader Joe's; instead, I always have a reserved parking spot right next to the front door. I also use the bike to ride to work on the hottest summer days, so I can quickly segue from my ride to my first meeting without needing a costume change or a shower. And exponentially increasing sales of e-bikes offer a clue to just how many riders are making the leap, too. In the end, we will wind up with a legion of new riders who perhaps hate traffic or worry about climate change and realize that bikes can provide a compelling way to take care of errands or commuting.

One of the best things about the transit riding boom is that the ridership is coming from two very different groups—people who hadn't done a lot of adult riding in the recent past and folks who already identified as passionate bike riders. This latter group is really interesting to me. Not that long ago, performance-oriented biking enthusiasts and utility riders existed in separate universes. Transit riders often saw spandex-clad road riders as dismissive of and disconnected from their realities, and roadies often looked down at or ignored casual riders or bike advocates. But the intersection of these two worlds is happening in a big way.

One thing that bonds everyone who rides a bike—from folks who do their best riding to the coffee shop in jeans to highly tuned pro racers who pedal for a living—is safety. Every adult who rides more than a little bit worries about getting hit. Whether they live in a big city or in sprawling suburbia or even rural farm country, they have well-founded concerns about the risks posed by speeding, distracted, reckless, or otherwise negligent drivers. This is the same whether one rides fast or slow, whether one wears spandex or cotton, and no matter the shape of one's handlebar or saddle. And especially because many fitness riders are increasingly likely to use their bike to run errands around town, the enthusiast crowd is finally getting more involved in advocacy, and the walls between transit riders and the enthusiasts are slowly but surely crumbling.

It is worth pausing to acknowledge that for all the progress that is being made, life for many utility riders remains more challenging than it should be. This is especially true for people of color. So many of the institutions that impact North American cities' progress toward being bike-friendly—the advocacy groups, the local government, the planners and engineers, even the established riding communities—are white-centric. Typically, the best networks for safe riding exist in white and affluent

Bicycles are magical and versatile tools that enable people to get around their community in a highly practical and enjoyable way. People who ride bikes have an appreciation of the gifts of passing through the world lightly.

---

communities. And often, advocacy institutions that serve riders don't seem to understand how safety issues for so many riders remain a problem when they get off their bikes.

Bicycles are magical and versatile tools that enable people to get around their community in a highly practical and enjoyable way. People who ride bikes have an appreciation of the gifts of passing through the world lightly. Bicycles don't cause traffic or pollution or require expensive fuel and upkeep, and they enable folks to squeeze a little exercise and fresh air and adventure into a simple trip to the store or work. Riding a bicycle on such utility rides is radically different than driving—rather than gazing out a window at your surroundings like a spectator, you become a part of the community, hearing and smelling and feeling everything around you. It is a meaningful and beautiful thing, something that should be accessible to everyone, especially those who feel marginalized elsewhere in their daily life.

It is easy for a conversation about city riding to devolve into polemics and issues, but the reality of daily riding is thankfully more joyful and engaging than that. For me, every ride brings little surprises, and I find myself in this blissful flow state from turning the pedals in easy circles, simultaneously connected to my surroundings and myself, my mind and body energized from the experience. All these things carry over to utility riding.

Cycling on the streets of Los Angeles and other big cities is often not relaxing, but it typically is exciting and demands that riders be 100 percent present in the moment. I have never once felt the desire to listen to music or a podcast as I ride because there already is so much to take in. I of course need to be attentive to what motorists are doing around me, but it's way more than that. One thing I love about Los Angeles that I can best absorb on a bicycle is the infinite tapestry of cultures and nature on display. I can ride by a playground and hear children shouting in different languages and smell the culinary flavors of the world. On my daily commutes, I have seen dolphins frolicking in the winter surf and inhaled the perfume of freshly cut grass and gardenias.

This, I'm certain, is a universal experience for people who ride bikes around town. Whether it occurs in a big city or a dense suburban zone or a small village, there's something cinematic

With transit and casual riding booming in New York, a bike lane on the Brooklyn Bridge opened in 2021, allowing this path to become a dedicated pedestrian zone.

about utility riding. Many riders have expressed to me that when they are in a car, they feel like they are passing through their community, a bystander in a pod, but when they ride, they feel immersed and integrated in that same community, a character in the narrative rather than a spectator.

For so many years, I found something wonderful in being out on my bike going nowhere in particular, and now I have found something equally wonderful in riding to somewhere I need to be. This is yet another reason why the bicycle is a miracle—it is a piece of fitness equipment and it is a toy and it is a kind of medicine, but it also is a remarkably efficient form of transportation and a legitimate solution to many of the toughest environmental problems our society needs to tackle. Some people who don't ride a lot imagine that riders are self-righteous, but the more honest reality is that they simply feel righteous—secure and content in the knowledge that they are doing something that feels good on every level.

I have long felt that people love bikes for how they can transport them to somewhere they need to be, but now millions of riders from every corner of bike culture are proving this more literally than ever before. They are finding something important while going somewhere specific. They've always known the meaning of the journey, but now they see the meaning of the destination. This utility, at once practical and spiritual, is why we ride.

Among the factors that have catalyzed a rise in bike riding in big cities are the widespread use of bike-share programs and the building of high-quality, protected bike infrastructure.

Chris and Melissa Bruntlett

Making Cities Around the World Better for Riders (and Everyone Else)

They didn't set out to be global evangelists for making cities friendlier to people on bikes. They didn't even set out to transplant their own family to a new continent. But when Chris and Melissa Bruntlett took a five-week summer vacation to the Netherlands in 2016, that's pretty much what happened.

Before that trip, the Bruntletts had pursued bike advocacy as a passion project while holding down full-time jobs in Vancouver, British Columbia. Chris was an architect, and Melissa was a communications specialist for an urban planning firm. From the start, they both understood the value of storytelling and content creation to inform opinions and action about bicycle policy and infrastructure. To that end, they had created the brand Modacity, a sort of creative agency to inspire more human-focused urban mobility, in 2014.

Then came the summer trip that changed their lives. The idea was pretty simple—visit five different Dutch cities for a week; meet with planners, riders, and community leaders in each city; and then produce a combination of text, photography, and video to document what

they'd learned. The experience was eye-opening for Chris and Melissa. They were not shocked to find that the Dutch cities were well suited to human-powered transport, but they were surprised to see how each community had faced unique challenges, perhaps due to its size or historical circumstances (like Rotterdam, which was leveled during World War II), and made different accommodations to find solutions that worked locally. They also were surprised to see how much of an impact the trip made on their children, who clearly felt a kind of freedom they hadn't experienced on the streets of Vancouver.

The content the Bruntletts published was consumed by North American bike culture, but they knew they had a deeper story to tell than what was possible in their initial digital project. So they dug deeper and in 2018 published their first book, *Building the Cycling City*. Combining success stories and hard-won learning from Dutch culture with case studies of innovative projects in North American communities, the book lays out a blueprint for cities to build a bike-friendly, human-scale future. The learnings aren't academic or abstract or idealistic; the book is full of practical, actionable approaches—how to link bike infrastructure with public transit, for instance, and how to build local political support for bike projects—to help cities adapt Dutch successes that reflect local realities. "It's too easy to dismiss the Netherlands as a bicycle utopia that's not achievable elsewhere," says Chris. "But that's not what we're arguing. We're convinced that cities can be better versions of themselves by learning from a country that figured things out years ago and is still working on them."

The Bruntletts went all in. The following year, they moved their family to the Netherlands—they settled in Delft, a small city located between The Hague and Rotterdam—and pursued ways to leverage social media and storytelling to spread the word. While many bike advocates are often understandably embattled or polemic, the Modacity brand is relentlessly positive and instructive and collaborative. "We don't want to just talk about problems anymore," Chris says. I find that reading or watching content from the Bruntletts is like cracking open a cookbook; I always feel that I will find solid recipes that have already been tested.

Living in the Netherlands broadened the Bruntletts' perspective. They now saw firsthand how cities that make smart accommodations to deprioritize cars and create safe spaces for bike riders wind up being more pleasant and livable for everyone. And so their second book, *Curbing Traffic*, explores the benefits of designing cities for people rather than cars. Melissa says the book documents how things that were good for people on bikes also improved other people's quality of life. Fittingly, the book pays special attention to the way women, children, seniors, people of color, and disabled people can more meaningfully connect with their surroundings on foot or on a bike.

Now the Bruntletts are in some ways transitioning again—from pure communicators to the mobility-curious masses to specialists directly helping cities around the world create actionable change. Melissa is working with a few organizations to help cities implement Dutch-inspired mobility solutions and foster gender equity in transportation. And Chris manages marketing and communications for the Dutch Cycling Embassy, a network of public and private entities that are exporting Dutch cycling culture to the world.

Although they are very much in the thick of their work, the Bruntletts have given thought to the legacy of their journey: "In the last ten years, I think we've been most valuable in diversifying what the image of cycling can be," Melissa says. "We want to show that cycling is something for everyone. Because when cities are better for cyclists, cities are better in general."

Phil Gaimon

*A retired pro racer who has become an
outspoken advocate for everyone who rides*

In the past, professional cyclists existed in a realm completely separate from that of people who depend on bicycles to get around town. But times are changing. For at least a few reasons—the pervasiveness of social media, the never-ending escalation of driver-rider conflicts on the road, and a long-overdue sense of unity within bike culture—a growing number of elite bike racers are embracing the urban advocacy movement and being embraced in return.

Phil Gaimon is a perfect example. The Georgia native was dominant in the US domestic stage-racing scene—twice winning the prestigious Redlands Bicycle Classic—and then in 2014 made the leap to the UCI World Tour, the highest level in the sport. Throughout his pro career, Gaimon got a lot of attention—for his climbing talent, his position on competing without using performance-enhancing drugs, and his ability to write about his experiences in magazines and books. In 2018, Gaimon announced his retirement from professional cycling—which turned out to be only partially true, as he transitioned to a career going after climbing records on the app Strava, an effort that includes a successful YouTube channel, sponsors, and intense training.

Along the way, Gaimon became a passionate and articulate advocate for everyone who rides in and around cities. For almost a decade, he has lived and trained in the Los Angeles area, experiencing the hostility and danger that riders face firsthand. "I've been buzzed and honked at so many times," he says. "At some point, I realized that I'm in this fight, too."

In recent years, Gaimon has used his substantial social-media reach and content platforms to speak out for safer streets. He has dedicated podcast episodes to the topic. On his social media channels, he frequently discusses the joys of utility riding and prods others in the racing community to get involved.

These days, Gaimon, who lives in the San Fernando Valley of LA, frequently posts highlights of both his world-class climbing exploits in the Malibu Hills and his casual errands around Los Angeles on his electric cargo bike. "I have a car, a hybrid," he says, when asked to describe his utility riding lifestyle. "But I purposely put a cover on it. Partially because I don't want birds to shit on it, but that's not really it. I live only two blocks from Ventura Boulevard. I'd be an idiot to drive for many of my trips."

When asked to explain his passionate pivot to speaking to everyone who rides a bike, Gaimon talks about his two-decade-long love for riding. He got into riding when he was fifteen—"I was a fat, depressed kid in Atlanta who was getting bad grades," he says. Then one morning he missed the school bus and had to jump on his bike to get to class on time. Soon he was riding that Huffy all over the sidewalks of Atlanta.

"Riding like that gave me my first taste of freedom," Gaimon says. "I feel that way still. Every time I walk out of the house to go for a ride, I feel born again."

Anne Hidalgo

*How the bike-friendly mayor of
Paris is changing the world*

For cities to make transformational strides toward being safer for and more popular with utility riders, it takes strong leadership at the top, someone who is unafraid of criticism and committed to change. And it's hard to think of a more impactful leader in this vein than Paris mayor Anne Hidalgo. Since taking office in 2014, Hidalgo has emerged as an outspoken champion and instigator of change in France's capital. She is demonstrating quite forcefully how one strong leader can transform the streetscape and culture of a city.

While North Americans may imagine that all big European cities are bike friendly, the reality is that Paris was for decades a sprawling car-centric metropolis, with persistent problems with pollution and traffic as well as complicated safety and quality-of-life issues. Within a year of her election, Hidalgo began addressing these seemingly intractable problems, not only talking openly about the intersection of climate change and transportation policy but taking decisive action, and the results are stunning—in both

their ambition and their impact in Paris and beyond.

In 2015, Hidalgo released her Plan Vélo, which aimed to double the number of bike lanes in Paris. While many mayors and city councils around the world have produced such reports, Hidalgo's administration has delivered on the infrastructure front. Bolstered in part by the pandemic, Paris now sees about one million bike journeys daily.

During her 2020 reelection campaign, Hidalgo advocated for transforming Paris into a so-called "fifteen-minute city," where residents of any neighborhood could fulfill all or most of their needs within the radius of a fifteen-minute walk or bike ride. She has initiated steps to remove more than 70 percent of the parking spaces in Paris and add roughly 180,000 new parking spots for bicycles. She has proposed turning the famed Champs-Élysées into a massive green space, banning diesel vehicles in the city, and taking other steps to shift Paris from a car-dependent city to one where bike riding (and walking) is a centerpiece of daily life.

This effort has not come without conflict or resistance. "There's been a very violent reaction at times," Hidalgo said in an interview with the *New York Times*. "Part of it has to do with [my] being a woman. And being a woman that wants to reduce the number of cars meant that I upset lots of men." But Hidalgo has fiercely stuck to her agenda and continued to transform Paris. And through it all, she has made a point to be seen pedaling a sturdy city bike in a sensible work outfit, demonstrating to all her personal commitment to the policies she's enacting.

The changes in Paris are having a worldwide impact. Because if a city like Paris, which long was the dominion of cars and not known as a haven for bike riding, can become one of the world's great biking cities, then such a shift is possible anywhere. Anywhere that has leaders with vision and the courage to fight for that vision.

"The situation is urgent, but I am confident because I know I am not alone in this battle," Hidalgo wrote in an essay published by *Time* magazine in 2019. "There are more and more of us fighting for a different vision of the world—a world that takes care of our most precious resources: the air we breathe, the water we drink and the places we share."

tamika l. butler

A pioneer in bringing social justice to the field of bike advocacy

Tamika butler was talking about the intersection of equity and social justice in cycling long before many folks in bike advocacy took the topic seriously. She was challenging urban planners and politicians and bike enthusiasts and pretty much anyone who would listen to see the inequity in transportation planning and do something about it. Then George Floyd was murdered by a police officer in Minneapolis, and the issue of social justice was suddenly at the center of the national conversation. And at last, everyone started listening to what butler had been saying for years.

Butler's journey to this position was full of twists and turns. She was born and raised as a military kid and spent many of her formative years living on a base in Okinawa, Japan, where riding a bike provided freedom and a cultural adventure. But as she got older—even when she was getting her law degree at Stanford University on a bike-crazy campus—she didn't do much riding.

Then, in 2012, she moved to Los Angeles and rediscovered riding. She got a road bike for the first time in her life and trained with a friend to do a big multiday charity ride. Riding helped her feel connected to the weird expanse that is Los Angeles. A few people told her she should apply for an open position leading the Los Angeles County Bicycle Coalition, the largest bike-advocacy organization in the nation's second-largest city. Initially, butler wasn't sure—she wasn't sure whether as a queer, Black civil rights attorney she'd be hemmed in by such a role—but she decided she could make a big impact.

She was right. Butler changed the conversation. She saw the inequities in how infrastructure is built in different communities; how bike issues and problems in housing and policing intersect; how the needs of marginalized communities were not being properly factored into the planning process. So she reoriented the priorities of the LACBC to center on race and equity in bike advocacy. She spoke out—both in LA and within the national advocacy community. She wanted people of color and other marginalized individuals to experience the joys of riding in a way that reflected the challenges of their lives off the bike.

"There are a lot of white, able-bodied cis men who have never experienced being marginalized until they got on a bike," butler says, referring to the systematic challenges of being unprotected, disparaged, and physically threatened that cyclists regularly endure. "I've tried to challenge people to see that for some of us, this is something we feel all the time."

Butler has since left the LACBC—she has a PhD in urban planning and is now running a consultancy business. She is hands-on in the transportation-planning process and speaking, writing, and otherwise influencing the conversation around social justice. "All these people who don't look like me are making decisions about our public spaces and how we get around," she says. "I want to make sure there are more folks thinking about this stuff."

It's far too early in her career to try to assess her legacy, but butler has already made a huge impact by persuading bike culture and city planners to see and feel the intersectionality of bike advocacy and race, equity, and social justice. Establishing a bike lane that makes riders feel safe is great, but creating communities where everyone feels safe and equally invested in progress is greater.

Butler and her wife now have two young children, and she feels that becoming a parent has sharpened her passion for the advocacy. "I want to leave behind something that's better," she says, reiterating her desire to focus on progress rather than fret over everything that needs to be fixed. "We have to decide what kind of ancestors we want to be."

Plentiful and well-designed bike parking is a key piece of the infrastructure puzzle that allows utility riding to achieve transformative growth.

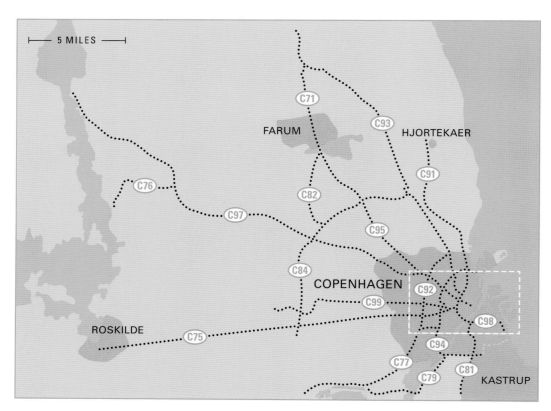

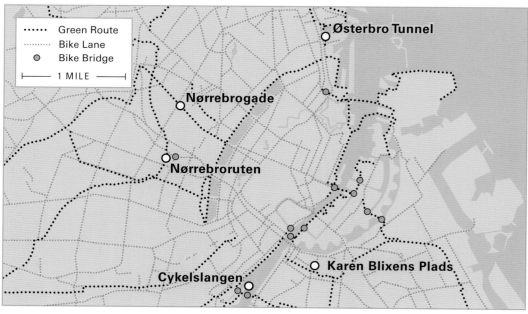

Live to Ride

Copenhagen Cycle Tracks

The Danish capital is justifiably fabled for its city riding

BY THE NUMBERS

- *50 miles (81 km) cycle tracks and other infrastructure in the city*

- *600 miles (966 km) paths and tracks in surrounding communities*

- *108 miles (174 km) cycle superhighways*

- *16 dedicated bike bridges and tunnels*

- *750,000 miles (1.2 million km) pedaled daily in the city*

- *650,000 bikes in the city*

- *120,000 cars in the city*

Denmark and the Netherlands are full of cities that have been built or rebuilt to make urban riding a joyous and safe experience. No city has been celebrated more than Copenhagen—through clever self-promotion and also an extensive and well-designed system of bike routes. Today, more than 60 percent of Copenhagen's residents commute to work or school on bicycles, and bike-loving tourists flock to the city for a taste of the good life. Copenhagen and its surrounding communities have hundreds of miles of so-called segregated cycle tracks—bike facilities that are protected from the adjacent roadway by a curb or parked cars. There's also a growing network of cycle superhighways—bike paths that are designed for more rapid bike transit into and around the city. And with spectacular bike parking, beautiful bike bridges, and some one-of-a-kind bikeways, it's easy to see why folks from other countries look to Copenhagen as a real-world paradise for riders.

- **Cycle Superhighways**
  As of 2022, Copenhagen had nine cycle superhighways—wide, straight bike paths that have few or no at-grade street crossings (meaning riders go over, under, or around busy roads so they don't have frequent stops) and are designed to enable bike commuting from communities surrounding the city. The network presently offers 108 miles (174 km) of paths, with a total of sixty superhighways planned to offer more than 640 miles (1,030 km) of high-speed commuting. The first route, C99 Albertslundruten, which is now used by more than four thousand cyclists on an average weekday, opened in 2012.

- **Cykelslangen**
  Literally translated as "bicycle snake," this architecturally stunning bike-only bridge winds and levitates more than 700 feet (213 m) over the city's harbor. Built in 2014 for a little more than $5 million, the structure has become so popular that more than twenty thousand riders cross it on a nice day.

- **Cycle Tracks**
  Typically one-way and at least 7 feet (2.1 m) wide, enough for two or even three cyclists to ride abreast, Copenhagen's cycle tracks are separated from the sidewalk, parked cars, and the roadway. The cycle tracks are plowed regularly in the winter. The route on Nørrebrogade, a downtown thoroughfare that was reconfigured in 2008 and now has a track that is up to 16 feet (4.9 m) wide in spots, is popular with commuters, casual shoppers, and awestruck tourists.

- **Green Routes**
  These are bike paths designed for recreational use away from busy streets. As of 2022, the Copenhagen region had roughly 40 miles (64 km) of these paths. The first such path, Nørrebroruten, follows an old railway line to connect neighborhoods without any car traffic.

- **Karen Blixens Plads**
  Located near the University of Copenhagen, this public park (named after Danish author Karen Blixen) has a large plaza anchored by undulating concrete domes that offer sheltered parking for about two thousand bikes. Generally speaking, Copenhagen lags behind other prominent European cities in terms of bike parking.

- **Østerbro Tunnel**
  While Copenhagen is justifiably beloved for its artful bike bridges, sometimes riders are asked to ride under obstructions. The most striking example is this tunnel, built in 2015, which goes under a rail line and provides an airy, well-lit, and extremely direct connection used by more than 2,500 riders a day.

The bike bridges of Copenhagen are like poetry you can ride on.

All-City Super Professional Single-Speed

Who says a city bike can't be fast or sexy?

The aesthetic details of this steel machine—classic lines, a lustrous paint job (with a special coating that prevents rust), and an elegantly crafted crown fork and seat collar— are stunning. But beneath the artful good looks, this bike is all business. The frame, fabricated from proprietary butted steel tubing, has the geometry of a cyclocross bike—meaning it's relatively nimble and rugged for a city rig. The entire setup is eminently flexible; it accepts tires as wide as 1.85 inches (47 mm), with mounts for front and rear fenders and stealth routing for a dropper post (which allows riders to lower and raise their seat without getting off the bike), and it is easily convertible to a geared configuration. This is not a bike for tootling to the coffee shop; this is a bike for folks who want to charge around the city. Or the park. Or wherever.

Live to Ride

Urban Arrow Family

This electric cargo bike will carry just about anything with aplomb.

A lot of people are turning to electric bikes to replace car trips. This versatile and surprisingly maneuverable cargo bike is more like a spirited two-wheeled alternative to a pickup truck or minivan. Whether you want to bring the twins to school, grocery shop for a Super Bowl party, or lug home supplies from the home-improvement store, this Dutch-made front-loading cargo bike can handle it all—even hills and rough roads—with verve and comfort. You'll get up to speed smoothly thanks to the endlessly dependable Bosch motor, and the Family is as good at slowing down thanks to powerful Shimano hydraulic disc brakes. A higher-end *bakfiets* ("box bike" in Dutch) is neither inexpensive nor lightweight; it's heavy-duty utility. But if you ride one as well engineered and spec'd as this Urban Arrow, you will be pleasantly reminded that e-bikes are still bicycles. Big-time fun is guaranteed.

Gazelle Classic

The epitome of Dutch style

Let's get something out of the way up front: This bike isn't light or nimble or technologically advanced.

That's not why you buy it. You fall in love with the Classic because it is at once beautiful and practical, regal and utilitarian, timeless and fashionable. It is the quintessential Dutch bike. It's as upright as they come— you feel like you're sitting

in a chair, with your hands closer to your body than on most bikes. Gazelle has been making bikes for more than 125 years, and it shows. You can feel at home pedaling this bike while wearing fine trousers or a flowy dress, because it has both the style

Alpha Pannier Backpack SMART

A clever bag for savvy commuters

Easily converting from an on-bike pannier to a backpack in seconds, this thoughtfully designed bag is a commuter's dream. It has padded sleeves for two laptops, reflective details and a rain cover, a helmet attachment, and plenty of space and pockets for all your clothing and accessories. The secret weapon is the optional Joey console, which allows you to charge your devices on the go, set anti-theft alarms, connect your phone to the bag via Bluetooth, find your location, and have LED lighting inside the bag. The 1,525 cubic inches (25 L) of capacity is enough to hold what you need to take to the office without being awkward to carry on your back.

to let you pull it off as well as a chaincase and dressguard to keep anything greasy off your clothes. Among the thoughtful touches that come standard: a front light, a ring lock, a rear rack, front and rear fenders, a multispeed internal hub, and both a handbrake and coaster brakes. You'll certainly be aware of the heft of the bike if you have to carry it up a staircase, but on the road you will feel stately, comfortable, and eternally stable. You will enjoy all that you see on a ride, including your reflection in store windows.

How America's first bike lane—in Davis, California— started a revolution

One morning in July 1967, a Davis, California, public works employee loaded a marking machine and containers of white paint into a city truck and drove over to 8th Street. It didn't take long to stripe both sides of a mile-long stretch of 8th. After the paint dried and stenciled lettering was applied, the small city had the first bike lane in US history—setting in motion an actual revolution aimed at giving bike riders dedicated places to ride in the street that has impacted every city in the country.

Davis, a flat, compact college town blessed with temperate weather all year round, was ripe for transformation. The first advocate was newly appointed UC Davis chancellor Emil Mrak. In the early 1960s, the university, which had recently been named the seventh general campus in the University of California system, was poised to have its student body expand from two thousand to ten thousand. Mrak was determined to encourage cycling to avoid an influx of cars. "I have asked our architects to plan for a bicycle-riding, tree-lined campus," he said in 1961, as an expanded UC Davis campus was being surveyed. Incoming students received a letter encouraging them to bring a bike to school, and officials drew up plans for a network of bike paths around a largely car-free campus.

Before long, Davis was pulsing with young people on bikes. But even though bikes were a dependable and fun way to get to class, many locals and city officials weren't keen on sharing the road

The University of California, Davis—located in a small city with few hills and temperate weather— already had a vibrant bike culture and was the perfect spot for a revolution to begin.

Today, Davis has more than 100 miles (160 km) of bike lanes and shared-use paths and twenty-five bike-only bridges and tunnels.

The protected bike lane installed on Sycamore Lane (top) in Davis, California, way back in 1967, was a transformational development for American riders.

with them. The police launched a ticket-writing crackdown as the tenor of bike-car conflicts grew worse.

Then Frank Child arrived. An economics professor at the university, Child had just wrapped up a summer sabbatical in the Dutch city of The Hague in 1963. There, he and his wife, Eve, had enjoyed riding around the city with their four children. When they returned to Davis, the couple sold their second car and soon thereafter wrote a letter to the local newspaper, proposing separate lanes for bikes on a few local streets.

The Childs started a vibrant organization with local supporters called the Citizens' Bicycle Study Group. The CBSG submitted a formal petition to install a handful of bike lanes. But their proposal was rejected by engineers, police, planners, and the city council, which held the power to authorize road infrastructure.

Hardly defeated, CBSG supporters sought change at the ballot box. Two pro-bike candidates ran for the three-seat city council—and wound up winning more than 60 percent of the vote in 1965.

Within months, the new council approved all the bike lanes in the original petition. But since California laws did not yet recognize bike lanes as a legal part of city streets, officials were concerned that they lacked the authority to set aside part of the roadway for riders. Fortunately, one city council member—a professional lobbyist in Sacramento—helped introduce and pass a bill in the state assembly. Governor Ronald Reagan signed Vehicle Code 21207, which allowed cities to establish bike lanes, into law in 1967. A few months after that law went into effect, officials in Davis installed lanes on Sycamore Lane, 3rd Street, 8th Street, and J Street.

In the early 1990s, Davis became one of the first US cities to install dedicated bike-signal lights. Today, Davis has more than 100 miles (160 km) of bike lanes and shared-use paths and twenty-five bike-only bridges and tunnels. Recent counts indicate that more than 33 percent of all teens in town ride to high school and nearly 25 percent pedal to elementary school. And all four of the bike lanes that were built way back in 1967 are still in operation.

NATURE

One does not need to ride singletrack in the Dolomites to appreciate how a bike can connect you to the beauty and restorative power of nature. But it helps.

I lived in San Francisco on a couple of occasions, and one thing I miss is biking across the Golden Gate Bridge. On some days, the trip itself can be less than ideal—it can be crowded or cold or frighteningly windy—but each ride ultimately ends up being miraculous in some way. On a bike, the bridge is like a portal to a new dimension. You begin on the edge of a bustling city and pedal into a universe with a radically different landscape and weather, a place where you can really hear and feel yourself breathe. A place where you feel more a part of the natural world than you did in the urban existence you inhabited a few minutes earlier.

Marin County is not a pristine wilderness, but it is a wonderland for people who love riding bikes. I've ridden hundreds of loops there, pedaling along a windswept seashore or through a forest of moss-draped trees or high up into a panorama of sky and ocean and chaparral. I have completed two-hour rides with 30-degree temperature swings. I have done some winter soul-searching in the rain there. And nearly every time, when I pedaled back across the Golden Gate, back to my home and daily life, I felt transformed, like something meaningful and medicinal had just transpired. People who ride know what I'm talking about.

This is, of course, not unique to one spot in Northern California. I have experienced similarly transformative journeys in so many different places. Along the Palisades of New Jersey and in coastal bogs in Maine and through the hills above Malibu and the rolling terrain of rural Tuscany. In the Utah desert and the High Sierra

I don't ride just to see the majesty of the world; I ride to be a part of it.

and the plains of North Dakota. I have felt it on rail trails and beach paths and dirt roads and even suffering through fast laps in Central Park. I did a couple thousand rides in Pennsylvania's Lehigh Valley over the eleven years I lived there and got that feeling on basically every single one of them.

I have been riding my whole life, and I can conjure so many experiences where my connection to nature felt visceral and pure. I remember one time when I was on a road trip with a friend and we pulled off the highway an hour before sunset to go for a short bike ride. We were somewhere in rural western Massachusetts. It was hot, and we started riding on a crumbly road that ran past a series of pastures. The sound of cicadas or crickets filled the air. The weather did not seem dramatic, but then in an instant, something changed. The sky didn't get dark, and the wind didn't pick up, but we could still feel a shift, a drop in atmospheric pressure and a thickness in the air. We looked at each other and said nothing but we knew we were about to get pummeled. Then a few seconds later, two horses in the pasture we were passing reared up and neighed louder than I've ever heard before or since. It was like they had the same realization that we did at the same time.

I have been passed on a big climb by a butterfly, and I have ridden by moonlight, and I have hit a chipmunk—it seemed to be okay—and I have smelled dirt kicked up by my tires in the desert and felt my rain-drenched jersey drying under a hot summer sun. I have paused rides to let bears pass and pedaled into a tree and admired the shadows and grayscale beauty of Flanders in March. I have seen thousands of sunsets on my bike and hope to see thousands more. I don't ride just to see the majesty of the world; I ride to be a part of it.

Modern life can be overwhelming. So many of us are consumed with work and family obligations. We are digitally immersed nearly every waking moment. There are video meetings and traffic jams and crowded supermarkets and endless emails. Many of us struggle to take proper vacations or find meditative moments or even unplug for an hour or two a day. And so taking a bike ride in a place where we are surrounded by sky and trees and have the sun on our back is more than training or recreation. It's healing.

Bike enthusiasts can find fitness and community indoors, but it's awfully tough to experience the full majesty of riding without being outside.

Being in a wild place, in tune with your surroundings, is a surefire way to feel more alive.

There is a growing body of scientific research to support this. And again, people who ride don't need to read the studies to know it's true. But digging into the science of so-called green exercise is pretty useful if you ever question the value of all those hours spent pedaling your favorite loop. Exercising in a beautiful natural setting has been linked to improved mental health. The greenery along the side of the road and the blue sky overhead and the birdsong and the smell of earth—researchers say that all these things help lower your blood pressure, stabilize the secretion of cortisol, and improve self-esteem. The positive effects can be measured after just a few minutes of exercise in a peaceful outdoor setting, and the impact is greater as you bike farther. People who ride and train for endurance know that it's considerably more tolerable to go hard and far outside than on an indoor trainer; that's because riding in a green space is pleasantly distracting and lowers the perceived exertion of such efforts.

But riding isn't the only way to chase these benefits—you could go hiking or running, for instance—but the bicycle is remarkably well suited to exploring wild places. You go slow enough to hear and smell things yet fast enough to cover a lot of ground. You can coast or soft pedal to recover; you can carry stuff without agony; you can fly downhill. With a moderate amount of training and preparation, you can spend the better part of a day riding through an ever-changing landscape. And even if you don't want to make that kind of time commitment, you can spend an hour cruising and smell the ocean or circle a lake or watch the sun set over a local park—simultaneously unwinding and exercising without any misery or hard labor.

For people who are serious about training or racing, the bicycle can transform a regular daily ride into an intense nature safari. You get in tune with the topography, the weather—especially the wind—and the sensory experience of being outside. You can bang out so many miles that you feel like a secret traveler, returning at the end of your ride with snippets of rustling cornfields or the late-day perfume of honeysuckle or an hour above the tree line or the theatrics of some nutty squirrel. This is, I think, part of why people love to watch the Tour de France—the spectacle of soaking in the individual moments and the totality of the French landscape. All those sunflower fields and alpine climbs beside tumbling creeks and the way that small towns dissolve into countryside.

Of course, a road bike can at times feel like an imperfect instrument for immersing yourself in nature. A beautiful and quiet paved road can disappear beneath your tires, leaving you open to embrace all the gifts that surround you, but too often there is traffic or development or angry drivers. Most cyclists diligently try to find the prettiest and safest routes in their area, but for a growing number of riders, it has gotten tougher to roll a bike out the front door or out of the garage and find peace.

This discouraging trend informs a number of seismic shifts within bike culture—the popularity of gravel riding, bikepacking, cyclocross, adventure riding, mixed-surface touring, electric

Riders know that sometimes you can go for a two-hour spin in the right setting and return home in a totally different place.

Weather
conditions
can shape our
experiences
on a ride. And
we often find
that dealing
with temporary
discomfort can
bring meaningful
rewards.

You do not need to be fast or highly skilled or willing to pedal to exhaustion to feel fully alive. You just need to be out there, turning the pedals, seeking experience and solace.

mountain biking, and indoor riding. Other than that last trend—the Zwift and SoulCycle phenomena—the rest are all activities and equipment that help people have meaningful outdoor experiences without the chaos of cars or the elbows-out personality of road racing. The purity of the experience can be distilled in a beautiful way.

Many of these emerging subcultures highly value self-sufficiency and community. These are styles of riding where your smartphone is not your most important tool. These are communities where sharing an experience with people carries more weight than beating them. Activities in which you still need strength and fitness but are likely more focused on exploration or tenacity than on traditional endurance. You are out in a wild place, in tune with your surroundings, looking to test yourself against natural conditions.

Electric mountain bikes remain a polarizing topic. Some people are worried about trail erosion and resource protection, while others are concerned that relative newbies will get in over their heads in remote places. But in large part that concern is actually driven by ableist prejudice—this idea that only very fit people should get access to ride in certain places. I feel that the positives of electric mountain bikes far outweigh the negatives, that getting exponentially more people to experience the rewards of riding on beautiful trails will mostly just expand and enrich bike culture. This idea that there's a purity to human-powered riding in the outdoors is pretty dubious if you consider the enormous amount of technology and engineering that has been poured into a modern mountain bike.

Bikepacking—or at least the activity that now falls under that rubric—has been around for decades, but the more recent uptick in popularity is fascinating. I used to backpack and even worked at *Backpacker* magazine for a number of years, and I think bikepacking delivers all the benefits of that activity (the freedom, the self-sufficiency, the opportunity to really get away) with the ability to go farther and carry stuff with less heartache. It turns out that the bicycle is an amazing tool for going camping in the wilderness.

One thing that all these unpaved riding disciplines and subcultures have in common is an appreciation of the terrain and the surface and all the technical demands that come with that. Nearly all roads in North America have been engineered so a big

Live to Ride

delivery truck or motor home can safely traverse them, meaning they are easily manageable for a rider with a geared bike and willpower. But on trails, riders must constantly be on the lookout for roots or rocks or changes in the topography or simply the nature of the ground. So people who mountain bike or otherwise ride on dirt or gravel wind up tuned in to the microcosmic world they are pedaling through.

But weather impacts everyone who rides. We spend so much of our lives insulated from the elements, sitting in climate-controlled offices and parking in indoor garages and getting food deliveries on rainy nights. By contrast, riding a bike in a committed way invariably requires some level of acceptance of temporary discomfort. And for many people who ride, grappling with this minor discomfort becomes quite manageable or even rewarding. Riding a bike means being out in the world, and so coping with a persistent headwind or a summer thunderstorm or a spring ride that has you transitioning from chilly to sweating in two hours can feel empowering. The equipment can handle it, and so can we. There are so many places in North America and Europe where cyclists persevere through pretty rugged winter conditions— New England, the Upper Midwest, the Pacific Northwest, and Scandinavia come to mind. I've lived and ridden year-round in Boston and interior Pennsylvania, so I understand how cyclists in areas where winter is no joke tend to keep riding with zeal. They do it because they love to ride and because it makes them feel alive.

The term *epic* has been beaten to death in the last quarter century, but the spirit that most people intend when they use it is a beautiful thing. Riders want to have intense experiences that test their mettle or connect them to a place or other people. They know they need to get off devices and find something way more organic to engage with. They want something deeper than to be a spectator in a wild natural world—they want to be a participant. They want to feel like an animal, just another physical being finding its way in a beautiful and unforgiving environment.

This is not to say that suffering is an inherent requirement to make that connection. There is a contingent in bike culture that believes that is so, and I think they are mistaken. You do not need to be fast or highly skilled or willing to pedal to exhaustion to feel fully alive. You just need to be out there, turning the pedals, seeking experience and solace.

Can any other machine transport people in so many literal and figurative ways? There's absolutely nothing wrong with riding indoors—it can be practical and efficient, secure, and even fun—but bikes truly shine when they carry us from home or a parking lot into the natural world, a place where our senses are fully engaged and we feel connected to something larger than our day-to-day existence. In this manner, something that started as a workout or a thrill-seeking adventure becomes something more like restorative downtime, a journey into a wild place that somehow leaves our lives slightly richer than when we set off. People who ride know what I mean.

Rebecca Rusch

The Endurance Athlete Who Became an Explorer

She no longer considers herself a bike racer, or even an athlete. These days, Rebecca Rusch, a living legend in the endurance cycling world, prefers to call herself an explorer. There are very few riders on Earth who are as committed to going deep—physically, geographically, emotionally, and even spiritually—in wild places.

Not surprisingly, this passion emerged in childhood. Rusch has fond memories of playing in the dirt in the backyard and of summer camping trips to different national parks. "Nature is where I feel comfortable and curious," she says. "It's always been about exploration for me."

Before her pivot to self-identifying as an explorer, Rusch was an athlete who enjoyed the outdoors while kicking ass. She won various huge ultralong races and numerous world championships and showed massive talent in multiple outdoor disciplines, including adventure racing, rock climbing, whitewater rafting, and cross-country skiing. The woman who earned the nickname the Queen of Pain was, in her own words, hypercompetitive.

As someone who already was doing extremely long and hard self-supported backcountry bike rides, she found that the transition into competitive riding happened smoothly. Rusch says that when people ask her when she'll retire, the answer is never. "Riding like this is not just my profession," she says. "It's my spirituality in some ways. And it's become clear to me that I need to be outside."

A breakthrough experience for Rusch was a 1,200-mile (1,930 km) bike expedition in 2015 through Cambodia, Laos, and Vietnam as she became the first person to ride the full length of the Ho Chi Minh Trail. It was an epic cycling trip and an emotional journey to find and visit the site where her father was killed during the Vietnam War, and her quest was the subject of an Emmy-winning film called *Blood Road*. Above all, says Rusch, that trip showed her how riding explorations could have deep personal meaning and lead to a spiritual immersion in a wild place. "I was riding through a history book while taking in jungle sounds, new birdcalls, and the sounds of machetes hacking through trees," she says. "You can't get that kind of feeling in your basement doing a ride on a trainer—technology cannot mimic nature in that way."

Since then, Rusch has gone on many more adventures—in remote wilderness settings, in rugged winter conditions, out there alone. She's had tons of intimate interactions with wild animals and says moose are the only ones that really scare her. Rusch says she feels more alive when her experience is dictated by her environment—waking with the sunrise, sleeping when it gets dark, making a fire when she gets cold. She's drawn to explorations in an awe-inspiring setting where she must be self-sufficient, and where the fear factor is real. The result? "These trips make me feel really small and really important at the same time," she says. "They demand complete focus and a complete lack of distraction. There is nothing else that you're working on. So you wind up feeling really alive."

When Rusch surveys how cycling culture has evolved in the past decade, she says many more riders are seeking a modest version of these experiences. She interprets the explosive growth of gravel riding and bikepacking as signs that people who live in a relentless digital age are trading their heart-rate monitors and structured training plans for peace and quiet. "People are gravitating toward what their souls need," she says, pointing out that scientists have documented how the color green, the smell of dirt, and the majesty of a sweeping view all release neurochemicals into a rider's bloodstream. "People know that their soul needs to be outside."

That's certainly the case for Rusch in her daily life. From her home in Idaho, she says, she can be climbing on singletrack and out of cell range in five minutes. Within that short span, she has a sweeping view of the mountains and is sweating and pumping her body full of endorphins. She's in tune with the earth, listening to the sound of her tires on the dirt, reading the lines of the trail. "I've chosen to live somewhere where I can get straight to the point," she says. "And the point is full immersion."

Sara Dykman

A wildlife biologist combines long-distance riding with studying nature

How far would you ride a bike to truly connect with nature? For Sara Dykman, the answer is pretty damn far. In 2017, the wildlife biologist pedaled more than 10,000 miles (16,000 km) over eight months—from the middle of Mexico up into Canada and then back, all part of a quest to shadow the annual migration of monarch butterflies. That journey inspired an award-winning book, *Bicycling with Butterflies*, and raised public awareness about a species in peril.

Dykman has been riding nearly her whole life. When she was a kid, she was drawn to the freedom that riding offers. She still feels that way. And when she got to college, Dykman discovered how cycling could provide community. "It's so easy to make friends when you're riding beside them," she says. Later, as she began bike touring, she discovered how riding could inform her interest in biology, advocacy, and stewardship.

Dykman's first big trip was a circuitous tour around the United States, visiting every state except Hawaii, with much of the route guided by animals she and her companions

wanted to see. In Florida, they rode 300 miles (480 km) out of the way to see manatees. She's also ridden the length of Central and South America to document frog populations and biodiversity on the continent, to really learn Spanish, and to otherwise seek adventure.

These long expeditions have taught Dykman to take a decidedly old-school approach to equipment. She tours on a weatherworn hardtail mountain bike—a 1989 Specialized Hardrock, chosen because it is not fancy enough to attract unwelcome attention and has wheels and components that are easy to fix and replace anywhere. And instead of panniers, she just mounts plastic kitty litter containers to the bike. They're big and waterproof and can double as seats and even be used to hand-wash laundry.

Her previous adventures prepared Dykman for her epic butterfly journey. That trip began at high altitude—at a nature preserve in a volcanic mountain range west of Mexico City where monarch butterflies winter. "It turns out monarch butterflies are perfect companions for a bike rider," she says, noting they cover about 60 miles (96 km) a day. She followed their migration route through Texas and the Great Plains and the Upper Midwest before arcing across eastern Canada into New England and the Northeast, ending her trip by crossing the Midwest and then heading back to Mexico. It added up to a grand total of 10,201 miles (16,417 km).

Dykman says that people often assume the hardest part of her trip was pedaling all those miles. But, she insists, bearing witness to the habitat destruction across North America that is threatening the survival of monarch butterflies was far tougher. These fragile animals have only one food source—milkweed—and Dykman's journey and book cinematically documented how human development has impacted the future of these storied insects, how cornfields and parking lots and relentless roadside mowing have put a species in decline.

Though she has completed some massive trips that might seem out of reach to many people, Dykman says she can find that same kind of restorative healing on a suburban or urban bike path. "People are just happier when they can feel the sun on their back and hear the birds," she says. "Nature is everywhere."

Still, Dykman says the trip was a meaningful and beautiful experience. The way she could viscerally experience the slow transition from desert to prairie in a way that's not possible in a car. The way she could camp out under the stars and pedal through a summer rainstorm and feel a genuine bond with the butterflies—just fellow migrants traversing a continent together.

Ronnie Romance

An influencer (and lover of wild places) who actually has influenced bike culture

It's too easy to call him an influencer. It's true that the man who would like people to call him Ronnie Romance gained notoriety through his perfectly rad Instagram account—for the uninitiated, it's @ultraromance, a stylishly photogenic celebration of unpaved adventure—but that would trivialize the genuine ways in which he has helped shift bike culture, inspiring people to rethink how and where they ride, what they wear, and how they interact with the natural world.

Twenty years ago, he was just another enthusiast on a road bike. He lived in Austin, he trained for performance, he did bike races. "I've been the cyclist in Lycra," Ronnie says. "I've been a serious cyclist since the '90s. Road racing in Texas almost killed me. I was doing intervals on a highway feeder road."

But then everything changed. He got passionate about tackling long backcountry rides way off the beaten path. He began wearing whatever the hell he wanted. ("I'm more into aesthetics than athletics," he quips.) At a moment when trends like gravel riding and bikepacking and adventure riding were gaining a foothold—and GPS-enabled apps like Strava were giving riders new tools to get out there—Ronnie Romance was the right guy at the right time to capitalize on the rise of Instagram and become the symbol of a legitimate movement within bike culture: namely, the rise of bikepacking. He was a guy with a cool beard and cool tattoos and jorts hucking on backcountry singletrack in perfectly lit compositions.

But a decade after his notoriety began, his quirky authenticity and legitimate impact seem in clearer focus. Now the word *bikepacking* is in the vernacular. Now way more riders have stopped chasing performance to pursue adventure. Now lots more people ride in nontechnical clothes. And now more people look to find themselves by getting lost in the woods.

These days, Ronnie lives in rural Connecticut, where he can ramble on two-hundred-year-old dirt roads and forage for mushrooms and pursue bespoke business enterprises like selling handsewn cycling bags. "I like riding on strange roads," he says, out of breath during a phone conversation while he rides on a strange road.

When I ask him to cite his most memorable adventures, the stories tumble out. About riding during a typhoon in Japan. About getting stranded on a mountaintop in New Zealand, a story that has a subplot about flightless ducks that kept entering his shelter. "I love immersing myself in nature and being able to connect dots on a map when I ride," he says. "The stuff in the middle is more interesting than the endpoint."

Gary Fisher

Decades after helping to invent the mountain bike, still obsessed with riding in wild places

If you want to start a heated but pointless argument, go to a dive bar in California's Marin County and ask old-timers who invented the mountain bike. People will make a case for the pivotal contributions of Joe Breeze, Tom Ritchey, Charlie Kelly, Gary Fisher, and a few other less-famous men. But the reality is that the mountain bike—a machine that transformed how cyclists can experience riding in wild places—was the product of collective genius.

Fisher, who sees himself more as an aggregator who refined good ideas than a solitary inventor, has spent his life building upon that quantum discovery. These days, he lives and rides not far from Mount Tamalpais in Marin, where mountain bikes and the culture around them first blossomed. Marin, a leafy and surprisingly wild corner of the Bay Area, has been home to Fisher since he was a sophomore in high school. "There was a time when I realized that I'd ridden every paved road in Marin," he says. "So naturally, I got interested in the trails so I could ride all the places in between."

This is not going to be a brief history of the mountain bike. That story has been retold many times. This is just a portrait of a guy who has loved riding bikes since he was a kid and has spent his life enabling other people to have fun.

Fisher caught the bug early. He was all in at a young age and his road-racing successes were pivotal to his identity. He entered his first race when he was twelve in 1962. He took an 80-mile (129 km) training ride that year from his home in Burlingame, not far from San Francisco's airport, looping all the way to Half Moon Bay and back. He spent an unusual amount of time during his formative years pedaling beneath redwood trees and into misty headwinds.

Fisher was on the long team to make the 1980 Olympics—which the US team would boycott—and he recalls racing and training with a young Greg LeMond (see page 65), who was just a "punk kid" back then. Fisher rode with LeMond and a few other racers from Marin to Los Angeles on training adventures. In many ways, the end of Fisher's elite road-racing prospects facilitated the full blossoming of his mountain biking influence. He recalls the revelation of his first ride on singletrack around Crested Butte, Colorado, doing 40 miles (64 km) alone on a 40-pound (18 kg) clunker. This and other experiences would help pivot mountain biking from an activity centered around downhill adrenaline to a culture that embraced cross-country adventure.

Now in his seventies, Fisher is still working, still spreading joy and inspiration. "I still do long rambles," he says. "I'm always looking to explore."

When asked to contextualize the impact of mountain bikes, Fisher is uncharacteristically circumspect. He'd rather talk about his love of riding in the rain or his joy in seeing older riders going farther on electric mountain bikes or the technical merits of different wheel sizes. "Between the scenery and the technical challenges, mountain biking demands all your attention," says Fisher, a guy who understands the value of unplugging from our busy lives and plugging into something more elemental. "Mountain biking helps you forget, and it helps you remember."

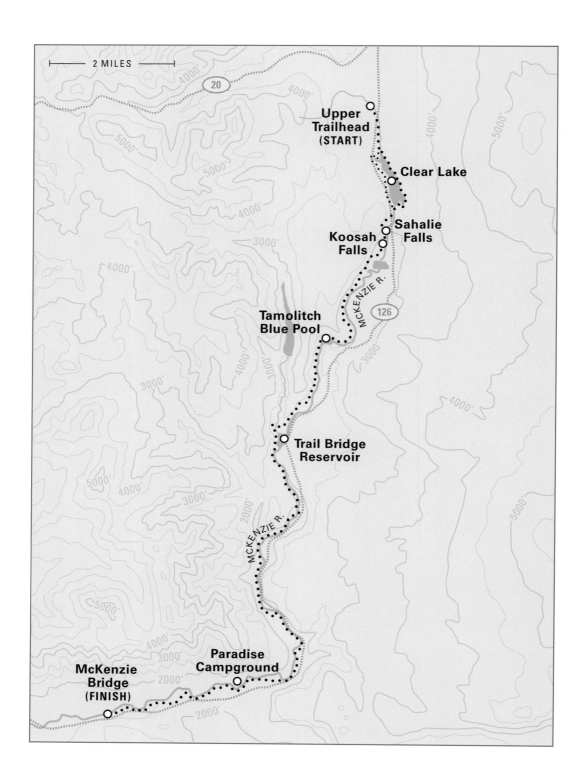

2 MILES

20

Upper
Trailhead
(START)

Clear Lake

Sahalie
Falls

Koosah
Falls

MCKENZIE R.

126

Tamolitch
Blue Pool

Trail Bridge
Reservoir

MCKENZIE R.

Paradise
Campground

McKenzie
Bridge
(FINISH)

Live to Ride

McKenzie River Trail

A flowy mountain bike adventure for your bucket list

BY THE NUMBERS

- 25 miles (40 km)

- 621 feet (189 m) climbing

- 2,329 feet (710 m) descending

- 40°F (4°C) year-round temperature of the Tamolitch Blue Pool

Located near Bend, Oregon, this 25-mile (40 km) trail is a bucket-list ride for good reason. The point-to-point route, which has more downhill than uphill, takes riders through an amazing range of natural scenery on the eastern slope of the Cascades. Riders cruise through lava flows and old-growth forest, past raging waterfalls and crystalline blue lakes. Figure on five or six hours for a one-way trip. Several companies offer shuttle service to the trailhead, including Horse Creek Lodge & Outfitters, which throws in a bike wash and a hot outdoor shower when you get back. The ride is well suited to intermediate riders, but it's manageable for many fit riders if they're willing to walk a few technical sections. All in all, it's like a rideable postcard.

- **Upper Trailhead**
  To take advantage of the downward-sloping terrain, most riders start at the northern end of the trail. The early miles take you through the first of several lava fields on the trail.

- **Clear Lake**
  Just a few miles into the ride, you'll cross a charming wood footbridge to reach this strikingly crystal lake—clear enough to see the bottom, which is more than 100 feet (30 m) deep—that's the McKenzie River's headwaters. You'll want to stop for a break, but since the water is a chilly 37°F (3°C) year-round, you might be more inclined to snap photos than to go for a swim. You can ride on the east side of the lake—which is more technical and scenic—or the west side, which is easier and still beautiful.

- **Waterfall Vistas**
  Past the southern end of Clear Lake, the route winds along the churning river and then crosses Highway 126 on one of the many charming handmade log bridges on the trail. On the western side of the river, riders will pass overlooks for Sahalie Falls, where water plunges 100 feet (30 m) over a lava dam, and then Koosah Falls, a 70-foot (21 m) cataract with a deep pool at the bottom.

- **Blue Pool**
  The river disappears underground for a few miles, and after following a dry creek bed, riders reach the most striking feature on this spectacular route, the Tamolitch Blue Pool, roughly 9 miles (14 km) into the journey. The word *tamolitch* means "tub" or "bucket" in the Chinook language, and when you see the pool, with steep sides and miraculously topaz water, you'll understand its name.

- **Hot Springs**
  Just a short distance off the trail, Terwilliger Hot Springs has five creekside pools, which range from a mild 85°F (29°C) to a scorching 112°F (44°C). Be forewarned: The scene is clothing optional.

- **Lush Life**
  After the Trail Bridge Reservoir, roughly the midpoint of the trail, the route leaves the river and cuts through three-hundred-year-old old-growth conifer forest, a shady playground full of moss and ferns and flowy turns. The trail is mostly smooth and relatively flat from here to the end.

- **Endgame**
  You know you're near the terminus of this beautiful adventure when you pass by the Paradise Campground, one of several Forest Service camping areas with potable water along the route. After that, it's just 2 miles (3.2 km) to the McKenzie Bridge trailhead and the end of this magical ride.

Weirdly pleasant surprises and moments to commune with nature abound when you ride in wild places.

Yeti SB140

A seriously fun mountain bike that's made to rip

In recent years, mountain bike subcategories have become increasingly specialized, allowing consumers to pick a purpose-built model that matches the trails and terrain and the way they plan to ride. While Yeti has earned a reputation for making superlative mountain bikes for serious racers, this trail bike is clearly designed to allow riders to have fast-paced fun. In other words, to rip. While the category has largely shifted to 29-inch wheels, the smaller 27.5-inch wheels on the SB140 make the bike playful and nimble. As with everything the Colorado-based company produces, the industrial design is clean and elegant; you don't need to see a big logo to know it's a Yeti. Thanks to Yeti's proprietary Switch Infinity suspension, the bike has an unusual split personality—efficiently navigating steep uphills and lustfully ripping steep downhills. It's not a bike for everyone, but if you find joy in improvising at speed on technical trail, the SB140 might be for you.

Crankbrothers M19

Maybe the best multi-tool on Earth

If you are going to ride off-road, you owe it to yourself to carry a multi-tool that is dependable, elegantly designed, and versatile enough to handle whatever goes wrong. The iconic M19 has great ergonomics, construction, and style—it's equally great to admire in your hand and to use while wearing gloves. The perfectly sized bits, made of high-tensile steel that will likely outlast your bike, include a chain tool, spoke wrenches, and multiple Torx bits and screwdrivers. If something goes wrong on the trail, you will be prepared. There are lighter and cheaper multi-tools, and a few with more functions, but none that are sturdier or better.

Santa Cruz Chameleon

A thoughtfully designed hardtail that's amazingly versatile

While riding a dual-suspension bike with more tech than a spacecraft can be magically forgiving, there are tangible joys to riding a hardtail. There's something to be said for simplicity. And the Chameleon platform, which Santa Cruz introduced way back in 1997, has always been about adaptability. The 2022 update can be set up with multiple wheel sizes, geared or single speed, optimized for hauling adventures or rowdy city riding or technical trail riding. The aluminum frame is exceptionally tough and offers a ride that is balanced and engaging. There's nothing particularly distinctive about the geometry or the component spec, but it's an exceptionally handsome and versatile bike for folks who love the refined purity of a thoughtfully designed hardtail.

How a 1986 adventure through rugged Alaskan wilderness showed bike riders how far they could really get out there

When Roman Dial, Carl Tobin (shown here), and Paul Adkins made a 775-mile (1,250 km) crossing of Alaskan wilderness in 1986, the word *bikepacking* was decades from existing. But it helped inspire a movement.

The word *bikepacking* didn't exist in 1986. For that matter, the concept that would inform the term—the idea of an ambitious backcountry wilderness trip on bikes—didn't yet exist either. But thanks to a groundbreaking and truly epic expedition in Alaska undertaken by Roman Dial and two companions, a trip that would be documented and celebrated the following year in *National Geographic*, adventure-curious cyclists got a sense of what was possible on a bike.

Like so many of the groundbreakers featured in this book, Dial got hooked on riding as a kid. Growing up in Virginia in the 1970s, he got a ten-speed when he was eight or nine. And by the time he was in eighth grade, he had a Bob Jackson frame made out of Reynolds 531 steel and was buying Campagnolo components piece by piece. He never had any interest to race, but as a young teenager he found excitement touring on the Blue Ridge Highway and the Outer Banks.

He first visited Alaska when he was nine, staying with an uncle who lived and worked at a coal-mining camp in the mountains. Dial fell in love with the state and moved there in the late '70s. His road bike wasn't very useful up there for most of the year. But when mountain bikes started to become more widely available in the early '80s, Dial—who was teaching environmental science at a university in Anchorage—began fantasizing about getting a bike he could ride to remote climbing sites or use to traverse glaciers.

The 1986 expedition—an unprecedented 775-mile (1,250 km) journey across the entire width of the rugged Alaska Range with

Dial, Tobin, and Adkins traversed the Alaska Range, which was chronicled in a big *National Geographic* feature that showed adventurous riders what was possible.

"Bikes are the coolest thing ever invented," says Dial, musing about the seven-week expedition and how thousands of bikepacking enthusiasts now head into wild places looking for a taste of adventure.

The bike makes you pay attention to nature.
When we ride, the wind and the nuances
of the terrain matter. And when we ride,
our bodies and nature are connected.

his friends Paul Adkins and Carl Tobin—was the product of that obsession. The trio rode titanium mountain bikes and carried inflatable pack rafts and otherwise traveled as light as humanly possible. They didn't even bring silverware; they ate meals off wrenches and other bike tools.

Dial and his buddies pedaled across glaciers and ran Class III rapids with the bikes on their rafts and rode on gravel bars and animal tracks whenever they could. "We called the glaciers 'slip rock,'" Dial says with a laugh. "The best was riding on buffalo trails. Buffalo avoid downed trees and leave beautifully buffed-out trails."

Dial, who has spent decades obsessively pursuing outdoor expeditions that satisfy both his passion for adventure and his academic interest in environmental science, says that bikes are his favorite way to travel in the wilderness. "You can walk almost anywhere—there's not really any creativity or imagination required," he says.

Roughly seven weeks after they started at the Canada–United States border, the trio reached Lake Clark National Park and Preserve. They had successfully traversed some of the most rugged and beautiful swaths of wilderness in North America. And thanks to a fourteen-page, photo-heavy *National Geographic* feature that Dial wrote, word of this new style of bike adventure spread far and wide.

Dial's escapades hardly ended with that trip. He's done big fat-bike adventures on Alaskan beaches and was part of the early days of gravel adventure riding during a stint living in California. He feels happy and maybe a little bit surprised that bikepacking has caught on; after all, when he embarked on those early expeditions, he was an eccentric trailblazer. But now tens of thousands of riders buy specialized equipment and pedal into the backcountry to find adventure and peace and a connection to the natural world. "Bikes are the coolest thing ever invented," Dial says. "The bike makes you pay attention to nature. When we ride, the wind and the nuances of the terrain matter. And when we ride, our bodies and nature are connected."

Dial, Tobin, and Adkins—who surmounted turbulent water crossings, perilous crevasses, and unpredictable weather conditions on their titanium bikes— forged deep connections to nature and each other on the trip.

COMPETITION

I have seen hundreds and hundreds of amazing bike races in my life. I've been lucky enough to have intimate access at the Tour de France and the Giro d'Italia, both as a journalist and as a VIP, talking with the racers right before or after tough stages, eating at the same restaurants and sleeping at the same hotels, shadowing the peloton on the road to see the action in a way that very few get to. I've been to national championships in multiple disciplines. I've been up close to bear witness as the very best athletes in the world explore their physical limits in the most important competitions.

But the purest, most beautiful racing I ever witnessed was in someone's backyard. It was called Fifth Street Cross, given that title because my friends Bill and Beth Strickland lived on a sprawling, woodsy property on Fifth Street in Emmaus, Pennsylvania. It began in 2005, and for that first year, I showed up as a spectator, chipping in to help with scoring or course management. After that, I got involved as a participant. It was too weird and magical to just stand on the sidelines.

Many people who ride bikes are familiar with the discipline called cyclocross. In it, cyclists race laps on courses that mix dirt trails, sand, and some pavement with obstacles like steep hills or wooden barriers. Even at the highest levels, the races tend to be about an hour or less—meaning the effort is more distilled and intense than in most disciplines. Cyclocross has been popular in Belgium and other European countries for decades and truly exploded in popularity in the United States in the past twenty years.

You don't have to race to enjoy the satisfying experience of testing yourself and finding community through shared effort.

We race to feel something. We crave experience and community. . . . We enjoy the feeling of going fast and the in-the-moment attention that racing demands. . . . We know that beer tastes better after hard effort.

From the start, Fifth Street Cross was not really like any other cyclocross race on Earth. I mean, it took place in someone's expansive yard after dark. Bill and Beth owned maybe 4 acres (1.6 ha)—they had a couple of tiny ponds, some pine forest, a small pasture with three goats, one of those giant wooden suburban swing sets with two slides. And all of these elements became a part of the course. At first, the only special equipment required was some kind of light. Even with a decent headlamp, it was pretty easy to get taken out by a branch if you were bombing through the trees.

Beer was a fundamental part of the competition from the start. Pabst Blue Ribbon—light and formerly déclassé—was the official beverage of Fifth Street Cross. A pretty sizable shortcut to the course was constructed, and anyone completing a lap could slam a PBR to cut some precious distance off their next lap. A strategy to attempt the shortcut every time in a five-lap race could comically backfire.

The range of talent that showed up for Fifth Street Cross included everyone from domestic pros and world-class track riders to semi-talented local enthusiasts to folks who probably did their most inspired riding to the coffee shop. At nearly all bike races, participants are sorted into categories that take everyone's talent, fitness, and experience into account, but in Bill and Beth's backyard, everyone just lined up and raced together. It was a circus of good cheer.

There were intentionally complicated scoring rules, created in a similar spirit as the PBR shortcut, that were designed to mock the traditional rigidity of racing and randomize or equalize the season-long standing. Coming in fifth had more value than finishing first. Having a horrible performance one week meant your score was subject to a better multiplier the next. These strange rules did nothing to blunt anyone's competitive fire to race well, but they did underscore the philosophy that nothing mattered more than trying your best and having fun.

One night, I got to stand on a podium next to Steve Tilford—a legitimate Hall of Famer in American bike racing, who tragically died in 2017—because he had won the race and I was being honored as the fastest slow person. Bill handed us both Schick razors as some sort of promotional gag, and I will always remember how Steve was smiling—not really caring about the win itself but just basking in the joy of being at such a ridiculously pure expression of what bike racing could be.

Competition is about community and our desire to have a memorable shared experience with other riders.

For most of us, winning isn't the real objective; the point is to work hard, gain experience, and have fun going fast.

It's a scientific
fact that beer
and pizza taste
best after a
really hard ride.

Let me get to the point: some insight into why the sporting side of riding matters and why bike racing is awesome and why competition is a fundamental piece of bike culture, even for people who have the good sense to do something else with their time and life force. So here's my explanation of why Fifth Street Cross was the most extraordinary bike race I ever watched or participated in.

What I am about to say does not apply to the very best elite athletes, who almost certainly were born with a winning Powerball ticket in the genetic lottery and then put in many years of hard work to hone their talents. For those racers, probably the Tour de France or a legendary one-day race or a national championship in their favorite discipline is the pinnacle. I get that.

But for everyone else, why do we race? In the end, I'd argue, we do it to feel something. We crave experience and community. We want to explore our physical potential. We find meaning in the struggle and the suffering and the occasional triumph. We enjoy the feeling of going fast and the in-the-moment attention that racing demands. We want our lives to be more interesting. We know that beer tastes better after hard effort.

Many people who don't actually race instinctively understand these things and find ways to tap into their competitive spirit without ever pinning on a number. Most recreational riders remember meaningful, happy childhood experiences on bikes—the distinctive pleasure of coasting down a big hill a bit too fast, the sustained work to get home or to school as quickly as possible, some senseless but joyful friendly competition with their friends. A bicycle is so many things. It is a versatile tool and a transportation workhorse and a means of self-expression and a vehicle for better health. But it's also a toy, a miraculous contraption ideally suited for communal play.

In the past decade, riders have increasingly found digital playgrounds in which to pursue this competitive spirit. In particular, two apps—Strava and Zwift—have provided new outlets for cyclists who want to test themselves and find connections. Strava, which came first, created a GPS-enabled social platform on which riders can track and share all their rides, find new routes, and gauge their performance on hundreds of thousands of segments around the world. So one does not have to ride with other people to compete with them. Zwift took it a step further, creating a human-powered video-game environment in which riders at home can ride and race with friends and strangers. Thanks to years of software development and explosive growth, riders can go on Zwift any time—literally 24/7—and find competition and community.

This combination of competition and community is what made Fifth Street Cross so special for me and the others who were lucky enough to participate in the early days. (The event still exists, though in a different venue and with different organizers and a more conventional format than before.) Believe me when I say that I was not good at it; there was one year when I had the goal to simply ride one perfect lap, and I did not achieve it. But the pursuit of that

Competitive riding demands absolute concentration, a welcome antidote to the digital distractions and endless multitasking that often define modern life.

objective—the effort to harness my engine and hone my limited technical skills and go as hard as humanly possible without falling into the goat pasture because I had one too many PBR shortcuts—was truly glorious.

To state the obvious, I have a fondness for waxing poetic about the glory of participating in competition. But there's another piece to this puzzle: the less kinetic but still intoxicating pleasure of sitting on the couch and watching other cyclists—no offense, but quite likely more talented than you—race bikes. In recent decades, technology has radically improved our access to such content. When I was an adolescent, it was basically impossible to watch any bike race live on television in the United States—even the Tour de France was run as an annoyingly tape-delayed and packaged human-interest event. Bike culture went through a decade when people moaned at length about "spoiler alerts" on Twitter because so many people could watch important races on cable TV only many hours after they'd actually concluded.

Thankfully, we're emerging from those dark ages now. While the streaming options for US fans remain annoyingly imperfect, an enterprising or free-spending fan can follow most big races live. The access for watching races is better than ever before.

Still, I'm not sure the glass is half full. The options for those of us who want to watch the best women in the world race remain massively short of adequate. Women's races are often still too short, the racers are paid way too little, and the TV coverage can be pathetic or nonexistent. But nonetheless, it's clear that change is in the air. And I'm totally confident that once fans get to see quality coverage of equitable racing, they will want to consume it weekly. It's mostly just a question of how many years it will take. Equity and representation are critical to the growth of the sport.

Watching a bike race isn't like watching most elite sporting events. Sure, you are watching hugely talented athletes trying to get to a finish line first with the help of teammates—in this way, the sport sounds pretty conventional. But if you tune in to an event like the Tour de France, you realize quickly that such standard sporting fare has been blended with the Travel Channel and WrestleMania. You journey from the Alps to the rugged shores of Brittany and see endless fields of sunflowers and platoons of tractors making art for helicopter shots and the infinite perfect villages that form the soul of France. And the event itself, literally created a century ago as a stunt to sell newspapers, is comically audacious. Who races 2,200 miles (3,500 km) in three weeks?!

This mix of absurdity and pure beauty and human suffering and glorious triumph has become part of the DNA of bike culture, something that connects nearly everyone who rides. People who are passionate about riding understand how all the weird and meaningful pageantry of life winds up connected to the bicycle. It sounds strange, but people who ride a lot know it's true. And so the traditions of competition inform bike culture in many ways. Racing informs the equipment and the fashion of people who never race. Riding a bike is in part defined by effort and community and playful fun, and it transforms us all into athletes. The act of turning the pedals, even languorously, binds us.

Still, the fundamental nature of competition is even broader than that. I'm thinking about one of the greatest races I've ever seen: a bunch of Japanese grade-schoolers on bikes that don't even have pedals. I still watch this competition once a month or so—I have it bookmarked on a Facebook page—to remind myself about something elemental that I feel about racing bikes.

Many riders know what Striders are—they're small children's bikes that don't have pedals. Some folks call the category "balance bikes"—they're an alternative first bike instead of a setup with training wheels. I think they are as cool as hell, teaching kids about the dynamics and fun of zooming around on a bike. It's more fun and arguably more useful than mashing pedals to go 2 mph (about 3 kph) on training wheels.

In just seventy-six seconds, this clip summarizes the weird personal and communal joys of competing. An announcer is shouting on a PA system, yelling "Go, go, go, go!" as twelve kids scoot off the starting line and then narrating the subsequent action in Japanese. There are inconsequential but spectacular wipeouts and more plot twists than in many four-hour races. These two kids wearing all black seem to have the race locked down, but this littler kid in white—who went into the first turn in last place—takes them wide on a late-race turn and cruises to victory. As he crosses the finish line, the little kid in white arches his back and dangles his legs off the rear of the bike in an oddly artful celebration. Parents gather round all the kids, and the camera remains on the line until everyone has finished.

The reason this short video has been viewed by more than 1.5 million people is the same reason why competition matters— why people race and why people watch races and why nearly everyone who rides relates to the odd pleasure of testing yourself. We want to feel something and be a part of something. People who race come to understand that there is only one winner and a pretty large number of not-winners. Still, they also usually come to understand that a palpable victory is earned simply by being out there, doing their best, simultaneously feeling their body at work and at play. Truth be told, I've never won a bike race, but I've learned that the pursuit yields something that means more to me than a medal: a more interesting version of myself.

Kathryn Bertine

Fighting for Women Who Race to Get Their Share of the Road

Kathryn Bertine didn't start out with any ambition to be an advocate for equity in sports in general. And bike racing wasn't the first (or second, or third) sport she took seriously. But circumstance and a tenacious attitude pushed her down a path where she became a powerful voice for change for women who ride.

It all started back in 2006. At the time, Bertine—who had competed at a high level in figure skating, cross-country running, rowing, and triathlon—was working as a journalist for ESPN and took a long-term assignment to see if she could qualify for the 2008 Olympics in any sport. Ultimately, her attempt to make the Beijing Games as a cyclist (for the island nation of Saint Kitts and Nevis) didn't work out, but it successfully turned her on to bike racing. She was hooked.

It took several hard, discouraging years before she got her first pro contract. She was thirty-seven at the time—ancient by bike-racing standards. But as she got more serious and passionate about bike racing, she became increasingly aware of an inequity within the sport that didn't exist in the elite sports she had participated in before. Women raced shorter distances and got paid far less. The races weren't televised. The rules that governed the teams were harsher. Bertine saw all these amazing athletes and the potential for a hugely successful sport—as well as all sorts of institutional obstacles standing in the way. Bertine was a professional athlete but had to work two other jobs just to make ends meet.

One final indignity pushed her headfirst into advocacy. As a former ESPN staffer with intimate access to the world of women's pro cycling, she pitched a short documentary for the network's popular *30 for 30* series on the inequity in women's bike racing and the fight to change it—and was rejected, told that there wasn't an audience for such a film.

So she crowdfunded, directed, and produced it herself. *Half the Road* debuted in 2014. Bertine says that people from sixteen countries—half of them men—contributed to the project. The film captured the spirit and excellence of pro women's racing and the obvious unfairness and sexism these athletes faced. "The film changed my life immediately," Bertine says. "It affirmed that what

I believed mattered. And it confirmed that the first step to real change was exposing the truth of what was going on."

I first met Bertine in 2013—I was at an event in Tucson with the actor Patrick Dempsey, and she elbowed her way into our conversation to tell us about her film project. Her fearlessness and passion made an impression on me. And obviously, she figured out bigger ways to elbow herself into the conversation.

Bertine was particularly outspoken about the Tour de France—without question, the most prestigious bike race on the planet. ASO, the company that runs the tour, has held a women's race in fits and starts since the 1980s without anything close to an equivalent event. Short stage races that were branded as a sort of women's Tour de France were held every year between 2005 and 2009 but ceased after that.

In 2013, Bertine cofounded an organization called Le Tour Entier (The Whole Tour) with three top pros—Marianne Vos, Emma Pooley, and Chrissie Wellington, all Olympic or world champions—dedicated to advocating for a women's race at the Tour de France and broader reforms to improve the commercial viability of the sport and develop a fairer future for racers.

The following year, Bertine and the other founders stood on the starting line in Paris for an ASO event called La Course. It was timed to coincide with the final day of the Tour de France. It was a victory in some regards. Bertine was at once gratified by the win and keenly aware that they hadn't really reached the finish line. The women wanted to race the whole tour.

From 2014 to 2021, while the men raced for three weeks on a 2,200-mile (3,500 km) course circling France, race organizers gave the women a two-hour race around Paris. "I believe that change has to come from the top down," Bertine says. "The Tour de France is the pinnacle of the sport. If it's not equal at the top, it won't trickle down. It's important that there are the same number of stages and distances. The way it is right now, it's like holding a marathon and making women exit the course at 9 miles.

The message goes beyond cycling. I mean, we're equals as humans."

There was more adversity to come—struggles that would help inform and fuel Bertine's advocacy. In April 2016, she was involved in a massive crash at a pro bike race in Mexico that left her with an acute brain injury. She spent weeks in the ICU and months recovering. She also went through a painful divorce and experienced years of friction for being the squeaky wheel—the pro rider who wasn't winning races but was speaking out for equity in the sport. The overall toll was exhausting.

But Bertine did not back down. In 2016, she created a nonprofit called the Homestretch Foundation. Using a large ranch home in Tucson, Arizona, as a home base, the foundation provides temporary housing, community, and other support to women who are professional or elite cyclists. In its first five years, more than seventy athletes took advantage of this program, a reflection both of how financially insecure many female pros are and of how much Bertine's work has made a difference. "My aspiration for Homestretch is for it to shut down because it's not needed," Bertine laughs, before quickly pivoting to the idea that the foundation could transition to help aspiring pros.

In 2021, fifteen years after her journey into advocacy began, Bertine published a new book, her fourth, called *Stand*. It's a manual of sorts, to help other people fight for equity. Her agent couldn't sell the idea to publishers. Much like with her film a decade earlier, she was told there wouldn't be consumer interest in her idea. So she self-published the book. "I wanted to share my journey," she says. "The good and the bad and the stuff that could help other people create change."

And that sort of change is happening. In the summer of 2022, a major step forward in women's racing was taken with the inaugural Tour de France Femmes—an eight-day stage race that took place directly after the men's Tour de France. The event, won by Annemiek van Vleuten, was an enormous success—with larger-than-expected audiences in person and on TV—one that likely would not have been achieved without the work of Bertine and her colleagues at Le Tour Entier.

Shawn Morelli

A Paralympic racing legend who embodies the real meaning of competition

Shawn Morelli's life changed during her first tour of duty in Afghanistan. Trained by the US Army as an engineer, Morelli was a passenger in a vehicle crash that left her with severe injuries—her neck and back were damaged, she lost the vision in one eye and most of the strength in her right leg, and she suffered a serious traumatic brain injury. At a low point, Morelli was suffering from PTSD, taking loads of drugs that caused her weight to rise. Her means of making a living and, frankly, her central identity—as a soldier—were gone.

In the unlikeliest fashion, she pedaled out of this bad place. Morelli says that in her Pennsylvania hometown, only young children rode bikes, but during her recovery, she visited a local bike shop and decided to give riding a try. It wasn't easy with equilibrium problems and no vision in her left eye, which meant she had no depth perception and was crashing into something or someone on every ride.

But she stuck with it, really just for fun and as mental and physical therapy. Morelli had been a pretty serious soccer player growing up, but she had no idea that she might have an aptitude for bike racing. In 2010, she went to the Warrior Games, and even though she wasn't formally training, she topped the women's field and finished fourth overall.

Four years later, racing in the C4 category (for people with lower-limb impairments), Morelli won her first Para-Cycling World Championship. It wasn't the culmination of her journey—it was just the start. Over the next nine years, she would win a staggering sixteen world championship medals (twelve of them gold) and a total of four Paralympic medals (three gold, one silver) in Rio and Tokyo. In Rio, she broke the C4 world record in the pursuit event. In short, Morelli became one of the most dominant Paralympic cyclists in history.

The purity of Paralympic competition is off the charts. Racers aren't there for fame. Many of them are there because they understand that lining up to test themselves has deep meaning. "Para athletes have such mental toughness, so much pain they probably had to overcome to even get to the starting line," Morelli says. "I have friends who are still on a morphine drip at a VA hospital. So for me, I think that getting to the starting line is my first victory of the day."

Morelli is aware that the end of her elite Paralympic career is looming ("I'm no spring chicken," she says, laughing), but she intends to keep racing as long as she can remain competitive. Because it matters—it matters to her, and it matters to all those whom she inspires. "Racing for Team USA means a lot to me," she says. "I went from wearing the flag on my shoulder to having it on my back. It has helped me a lot mentally and emotionally. I've found freedom through bike racing."

Justin Williams

An innovator (and elite sprinter) bringing equity to bike racing

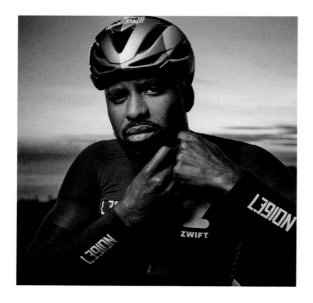

Justin Williams doesn't just want to win bike races. He wants to change the sport. And he's succeeding.

Williams was born and raised in South Los Angeles. He acknowledges that very few kids in South LA imagined themselves racing bikes—it was an activity that existed in a distant universe. But his family is from Belize, which has a rich cycling culture. And when he was thirteen, he convinced his dad to help him get into the sport. He learned firsthand that riding bikes can be very hard.

Achieving equity in competitive cycling is also tough. Bike racing, especially in the United States, has not historically been a paragon of representation. It's safe to say that the sport hasn't done a stellar job reaching young Black people. But in Southern California, things are really starting to change. Williams and his brother, Cory, also a successful professional racer, have emerged in the last five or six years as dominant forces in the distinctively American discipline of crit racing. For those who don't

know the criterium discipline well, these races involve multiple laps on a closed course. They typically last an hour or two—significantly shorter than a road race at the same level—and the courses tend to be relatively flat, relentlessly fast, and full of sharp turns.

The path to the highest level of the sport did not come easily for Williams. After showing a lot of early promise, he was invited as a teenager to join a prestigious development team in Europe. But despite some promising results in races, he struggled. It can be tough for any young athlete to adjust to a new culture, but the European racing scene was particularly unwelcoming to a young Black man from South LA.

But after some ups and downs, Williams found his groove. The big breakthrough came in 2018, when, racing as a sort of privateer without a conventional pro team contract, he finished in the top three in a remarkable thirty out of thirty-five races and won national championships in both the criterium and road race. As an elite racer, Williams was really on the map—winning important races with style and racecraft and world-class finishing speed.

But he wanted more than that. "It's not enough for me to just do something on my own," Williams told me in a 2020 interview. "I need to create something, to grant opportunities to people I love who I know deserve it." So he and Cory formed their own team. They called it L39ion—with a typographical play on 39th Street in South LA, where they grew up. With a pro men's team, an elite women's team, and a development squad, L39ion assembled a diverse collection of riders unrivaled in the sport. But the team made waves with results, too—L39ion riders won some of the biggest criteriums in the United States and various national championships in Belize, Mexico, Barbados, and the States.

Still, Williams has even bigger dreams—to evolve and grow the distinctly American discipline of criterium racing. In 2023, he helped launch a new racing league in which teams compete in major markets. He also wants to build race courses in these cities that would provide a venue for young people of color to get into bike racing. "It's never seemed clearer what I'm trying to accomplish—to attract younger people from different backgrounds to the sport," Williams said. "This is bigger than me or the team."

Tim Johnson

A lifetime dedicated to the joy of racing in multiple disciplines

Tim Johnson *is* bike racing.

In 2017, I wrote a feature that feted a rare breed of bike racer—the lifer. These are people who compete for decades in multiple disciplines, people who give as much to the sport as they take from it, people whose passion does not wane as they age. "Real cyclists ride more than one kind of bike," Johnson told me.

He was talking about another racer, but he could have been talking about himself. Johnson showed the most talent and had the most success in the discipline of cyclocross—he won six elite US national titles and represented the United States at the world championships thirteen times—but he began as a mountain biker and competed as a pro road racer at the highest level for many years. ("Road racing is

like hot sauce," Johnson says. "Not everyone has a taste for it.")

Johnson grew up in Massachusetts and got his first real bike when he was fifteen. After spending the summer helping a neighbor—a diabetic who'd had a bad fall—Johnson was gifted a new mountain bike. And by chance, he went into a local bike shop and saw a flyer for a race a week away. Participating in it would change his life, giving him an identity, a community, a passion. "Racing gave me a social base," he says. "I was riding a lot. My parents were going through a divorce. I made all these great friends, and we spent a lot of time together training and driving to events."

Johnson, who raced all sorts of bikes for twenty-plus years, is philosophical about why he loves competition so much. "Man, when you're racing and you realize that the other riders are out of your control, you get into this flow state. All you're doing is managing the moment. Competition really drills things down to that. It can be narcotic, euphoric."

For a long time, even before he retired, Johnson was involved in bike culture. He worked tirelessly as an advocate for organizations like People for Bikes and MassBike, raising money and awareness for rider safety. And not long after his retirement, Johnson joined the USA Cycling Foundation—the philanthropic arm of the sport's governing body in the United States, focused on supporting young talent and grassroots efforts to build the sport—as development director.

Johnson wants bike racing to grow and diversify in the United States, to see people come from demographics that didn't used to be a part of the sport and find a new home. And though he'd like to help discover and support future national champions, he also wants a much larger group of people to find community and pursue new challenges and fall in love just like he did.

"The community you can find in bike racing is really strong," Johnson says. "You get close with all these other riders as you experience adversity, success, and difficulty. I definitely want to share that with people."

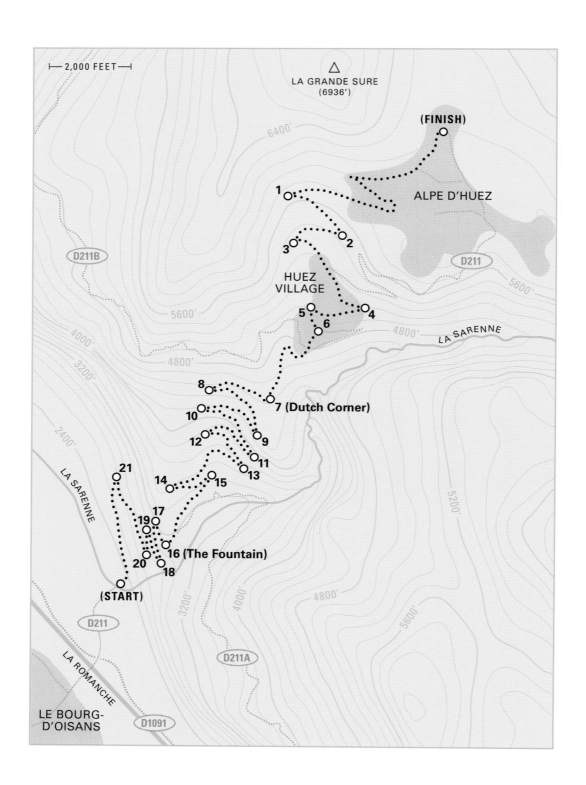

Live to Ride

Alpe d'Huez

Perhaps the most iconic climb in Tour de France lore, the switchbacks of Alpe d'Huez beckon everyone to rise to the challenge

BY THE NUMBERS

· *8.6 miles (13.8 km)*

· *Elevation: 2,539 feet (774 m) at the base; 5,955 feet (1,815 m) at the traditional Tour de France finish*

· *21 switchbacks*

· *Average grade: 8.1 percent*

· *Steepest grade: 13 percent*

There are longer and harder climbs that appear in the Tour de France, but none is more celebrated than Alpe d'Huez. The 8.6-mile (13.8 km) climb in the Alps takes riders up twenty-one switchbacks and 3,500 feet (1,067 m) to arrive in the modest ski village. Racers in the Tour have ascended the winding climb, which can be jammed with roughly one million fans, more than thirty times since the 1950s. The climb is well suited for roadside fans and televised drama, but the most visceral way to experience it is to ride it yourself.

• Most riders begin in the small commune of Le Bourg-d'Oisans, which is packed with cafés and bike shops. The first five minutes of the ride are the only flat roads you'll encounter.

• Generally speaking, the twenty-one turns are the easiest stretches. The steepest stretch comes between turns 9 and 8, halfway up the climb. There are also tough pitches at the bottom around turn 21 and after turn 5 and the village of Huez.

• Don't pass up filling your water bottle at the fountain on turn 16.

• Turn 7 is celebrated as Dutch Corner. During the Tour, this sweeping bend turns into a pulsating sea of orange-clad fans from the Netherlands, who have decamped here since the 1960s. Typically, the pavement is painted orange, and the air smells like beer and a couple of less pleasant aromas.

• Each of the turns is marked with a sign that celebrates the riders' progress and bike racers who have triumphed on Alpe d'Huez, including legends like Fausto Coppi, Marco Pantani, Bernard Hinault, and American Andy Hampsten.

• The end is near when you pass the stone church of Saint Anne, about a mile (1.6 km) below the village of Alpe d'Huez.

• Purists finish the climb on Avenue du Rif Nel, near the base of the ski slope. The fastest pros have ridden the climb in less than forty minutes, but merely pedaling the whole thing is a victory for many recreational riders.

Colnago C68

A modern race bike made with a heritage of craftsmanship

There are numerous brands that produce race bikes with history, technical excellence, or extraordinary artistry, but if you want a race bike with all three, Colnago is really in a class of its own. Ernesto Colnago, who turned ninety in 2022, is still overseeing the workshop beneath his home in a small town near Milan called Cambiagio. He has built bikes for champions for six decades now. He once told me that "the frame of the bicycle is like the heart." It is hard to think of a contemporary race bike with more heart than the Colnago C68. A thoroughly modern replacement for the legendary, lugged C64,

Live to Ride

Selle Italia SLR Kit Carbonio

An ultralight bike saddle that makes zero compromises

Choosing a bike saddle for racing typically involves trade-offs. Is your priority comfort or weight? Are you passionate about ergonomics or aerodynamics or aesthetic beauty? If you are willing to invest in the SLR Kit Carbonio—it doesn't come cheap—the answer can be all of the above. That's why it's been a longtime favorite of pro racers. With ceramic-coated carbon rails and a minimalist design, this saddle weighs a mere 122 grams—about a quarter of a pound. It's far from cushy, but it's comfortable for long, hard rides, it's highly aerodynamic, and it oozes classic Italian style.

the C68's sleek carbon fiber frame (with less obvious 3D printed lugs) delivers a lot of adjectives—it's light, stiff, lively, aerodynamic, and powerful. The C68 demands and rewards the attention of a skilled rider and is remarkably stiff and responsive without being harsh or overly reactive. The detailing—the paint and the obsessively thoughtful tubing—is impeccable. It's not a bike for everyone. But maybe it's a bike for you.

How Zwift changed the game

Zwift cofounder
Eric Min always
believed that
the platform
could change the
nature of cycling
competition,
but even he is
surprised that
users have
pedaled more
than 2.5 million
miles.

Eric Min and Jon Mayfield had never met and they lived on different continents, but both were struck by the same thought: Training indoors on a bike isn't fun. Mayfield recalls trying to ride on a trainer while watching Netflix and realizing quickly that it wasn't going to work. That kind of shared gripe brought the two strangers together in 2013 to launch a start-up that has changed how people ride.

Min and Mayfield's disruptive desire to create an engaging digital cycling experience led to the birth of Zwift, a multiplayer game that lets cyclists train, interact—and, more recently, compete—in the virtual world. The immersive environment allows players to join group rides with other cyclists and use smart trainers to measure their performance and determine their rank in the game.

At a time in which nearly every aspect of modern life has found a digital expression, it shouldn't be surprising that competitive bike riding would carve out a virtual existence. But the vitality of the community participating in this universe seemed unimaginable five years ago. Though riding seemed to be defined by a sense of place and terrestrial company, it turned out that a cycling video game could become genuine social media.

I first met Min and Mayfield in 2018, at Zwift headquarters in Long Beach, California. At that point, the company had established itself as a dominant platform for cyclists to train together and find community, but the ambition to become a legitimate force in competition was still in its infancy.

But by the end of 2021, many of the start-up platitudes that Min had uttered a few years earlier had come true. That year, more than seven hundred professional bike racers—and hundreds of thousands of aspiring amateur racers—competed in digital competitions on Zwift. In December 2020, the first-ever Cycling Esports World Championships sanctioned by the UCI, the governing body for all elite cycling, was held on separate 50-kilometer (3.1-mile) courses for men and women—all of it managed by Zwift.

If you aren't one of the three-million-plus paying Zwift customers (or a fan who's watched live races), here's how it works in a nutshell. To get started, riders need a setup with three key components—a bike, a trainer that holds the bike and helps collect data, and a device (namely, a smartphone, tablet, or computer) that runs the Zwift software. Then you join a ride; onscreen, your avatar is out on the road with other participants, completely powered by your effort on the trainer.

The growth of this community is staggering. There are now paid participants in more than 190 countries using the platform. Together, these riders have pedaled more than 2.5 billion miles (4 billion km) in the digital world. During 2021, these folks challenged themselves or competed in more than 110,000 events. And in 2022, the company launched new functionality for clubs—so riders in the digital space can ride and train just with their friends like they do IRL.

Clearly, what began as a way to make riding indoors in bad weather fun has turned into something far bigger than that. Not surprisingly, Zwift flourished during the pandemic, as enthusiasts sought new, safe ways to find community and competition.

Racing in the digital world isn't just a substitute for racing outdoors; it has certain advantages that open the sport to a wider demographic—people who live in rural areas or cultures where bike racing isn't very popular or accessible. And, as Min notes, traditional forms of bike racing have been extremely intimidating to newbies. Many cyclists literally spend years training and understanding the culture before they enter their first race. By contrast, joining a digital competition on Zwift is considerably easier and safer—and no less rewarding.

For those who ride to build fitness or seek competition, cycling is an extremely data-driven sport. A rider can easily measure their progress and formulate a training plan based on this kind of data. "And in the digital world, the sport is even more data-driven," says Min. "Riding on Zwift is like riding in a lab."

Zwift has even changed the nature of competition, finding new ways to lure riders to challenge themselves and validate their performance. Zwift users can of course participate in digital races, but they also can achieve new levels of competition or collect badges—familiar signposts in the world of video games but a new intoxicant for amateur athletes.

Min says he fully expects Zwift racing to be an Olympic sport by 2028. It sounds like start-up hyperbole. But I wouldn't bet against it.

Min, who still likes to ride outdoors, believes that Zwift can expand the demographics of people who want to experience the social and competitive nature of the sport.

SELF-EXPRESSION

There is so much beauty in the act of riding a bicycle. The bike itself can be an object of desire or individuality, and there is grace in the physical activity. You are spinning circles, in flight and fully alive and in tune with your machine. You are part of something larger, connected to a meaningful heritage. These things are true whether you are slicing through singletrack or cruising in jeans to the coffee shop or drilling it on a fast-paced group ride.

The bicycle is such a versatile tool, able to help us do so many things, and one of them is to assert something unique and beautiful about ourselves. This can be done in physical ways—through the style of your bicycle, or how you interpret fashion (or flout it) in your riding, or in the personality you bring to your cycling. It also can be done on a metaphysical level—how you learn to welcome and embrace people and passions that expand the perimeter of bike culture. This means that self-expression, while deeply individualistic in obvious ways, also engenders a culture of tolerance.

Many people who care deeply about bikes realize that all the important social issues of our time—racism, poverty, gender inequality, sexuality, housing and transportation equity, policing, trans rights, body image, even climate change—intersect with bike culture in one way or another. Sure, some recreational enthusiasts who simply look at a bike as a piece of sporting equipment might not yet be wrestling with this, but I see generational change happening as new communities of riders with a deep desire to be themselves, to be heard and seen and respected, are being embraced.

Mountain bike industry veteran Jeff Kendall-Weed artfully hucks his bike off a concrete cistern on the 5,066-foot (1,544 m) summit of Mount Lukens, the highest point in the city of Los Angeles.

Wear what you want. Ride what and where and how you want. In the end, style is not about conforming to a code—it's about expressing your personality. And self-expression is ultimately about being true to yourself.

Broadly speaking, the contours of mainstream bike culture are being reshaped by seismic shifts. Riders in North America have long been drawn to the deeper beauty and fabric of the culture, particularly as it relates to riding in Europe, but now I see a distinct transformation unfolding. Nothing here is binary—but there's a move away from conformity and toward self-expression. And the way it is unfolding in the United States, where all sorts of social change and self-examination are underway, is thoroughly unique.

Certain flavors of self-expression have been celebrated in bike culture for a long time. Many riders have little interest in the traditional sporting aspects of cycling, never mind the history of the sport. Nonetheless, that historical narrative adds texture to modern bike culture. Many of the most legendary bike racers of the past seventy-five years—Fausto Coppi, Jacques Anquetil, and Eddy Merckx come to mind—were like golden age movie stars, transcending pure sport through their style and grace and flair and audacity. Such riders are celebrated for their panache, the way they could express highly personal verve on and around the bike.

But this heritage of self-expression transcends racing. I've visited Europe many times on bike-related business, and these trips have altered how I think about bike culture—about the traditions and modern realities and possibilities that shape the world for people who ride. Nothing against the amazing bike-related experiences I've had in France and Belgium, two heartlands of bike culture, but my trips to Italy have more viscerally influenced the self-expression that centers my riding life.

I will always remember visiting a factory in Bressanvido and watching local villagers make beautiful Fizik and Selle Royal saddles by hand. In the middle of the day, all the laborers walked or rode a bike home for a couple of hours. I eventually saw firsthand how many of my favorite Italian bike products emerge from such a setting, crafted artfully by people for whom bikes sit at the axis of an interesting and well-balanced life. These objects are not simply manufactured durable goods; they are objects of love.

Down in Treviso, I visited Pinarello HQ several times. This was back when Giovanni Pinarello, the founder of the brand, was still alive. The old man hung around the brand's flagship store, usually

You don't need to be a fan of racing to see how modern bike culture has been enriched by the grace of golden era greats like Eddy Merckx (*opposite*) and Fausto Coppi.

1997   Road Hub
mock up / Prototype
shown in
Copper Penny

with a pink sweater carefully knotted around his shoulders, eager to project warmth toward anyone who came in to adore the bicycles bearing his name. Elsewhere in Treviso, which coincidently is also where Benetton is based, I saw elderly couples tootling around town on bikes, dressed in an effortless style that is common in this part of Italy. It was impossible to overlook the cultural value of bikes there, as objects of authentic personal meaning.

And up near Trento, I got to visit with legendary framebuilder Dario Pegoretti. Pegoretti, who sadly died in 2018, was many things—an artist, a technician, a humanist, a poet/comedian. Early in his career, he was a builder of trust for some of the best professional racers in the world, and later he made bikes for people who wanted something wildly individualistic. It would be myopic to lionize his bikes solely for their aesthetics—because Pegoretti built uncompromising purpose-driven machines that won the biggest bike races on the planet—but nonetheless, he deserves recognition for how he painted bikes with audacious panache. They are rideable art. Through his work, Pegoretti proved that a high-end bike could also be high-performance art. That someone could build a bicycle that is at once meticulous sporting equipment and an existential statement about individuality.

When I knew Pegoretti, he had overcome Hodgkin's lymphoma and thus was as joyously unfiltered and in the moment as anyone I've met in my life. I don't really have many bike-related regrets in my life, but one of the biggest is that he measured me for a frame—it was late morning and he was smoking and drinking red wine and listening to Coltrane's album *Lush Life*, and we discussed the idea of him painting a frame loosely inspired by the track "Like Someone in Love"—but due to cash-flow worries, I never ordered the bike.

Of course, Pegoretti is hardly the only interesting framebuilder in the bike universe. Over the past twenty years, there's been an enormous renaissance in the art and business of custom bikes. In 2005, Don Walker organized the first North American Handmade Bicycle Show in Houston, and since that intimate gathering, NAHBS grew into a major consumer and community event (see page 198). The idea of getting a custom-made bicycle, which was a very niche fantasy twenty-five years ago, now has far broader appeal. There are a few extraordinary builders and a number of talented and creative builders and a bunch of aspirants. It's a multilayered community. The central philosophy of the handbuilt movement is that bikes can be lovingly and mindfully fabricated to match the size, needs, desires, and personality of one person. These bikes are made by a craftsperson rather than at a factory. It's this idea that the right bike for you does not come out of a mold, literally.

I went to NAHBS for the first time in Austin in 2011. So I was a little late to the party. The handbuilt movement was being buoyed by broad shifts in both cycling and the larger culture. People were increasingly interested in buying produce and other products that were grown, sourced, or made locally. Businesses like independent coffee shops and gastropubs were booming. Digital businesses like Etsy, which created new markets out of consumer interest in

Bikes hanging in the workshop at Rock Lobster (*top*). A copper-plated hub from the early years of Chris King's career (*bottom*).

The handbuilt movement lets riders own a bike that reflects their individuality and riding style. Shown here: a randonneur bike and trailer made by the small Santa Cruz–based builder, Francis.

The gravel riding phenomenon has helped bring sorely needed nonconformist style and casual community spirit to bike racing.

distinctive noncorporate craft and clothing, blew up. Artisanship was regaining prestige in our culture after waning for many decades. Meanwhile, casual riding in cities was growing exponentially, as a far wider demographic than traditional cycling enthusiasts started exploring and interacting with their communities on a bike. Road racing was in decline as cyclocross was booming. A lot of enthusiasts started feeling disillusioned about pro racing and maybe also about the brands that sponsored certain riders.

The handbuilt community benefited from all these developments. Entirely new categories of bikes—fat bikes, gravel bikes, adventure bikes—have emerged or found early traction from the makers at NAHBS and their ilk. Of course, some builders specialize in performance, but in general, the bigger bike brands are designing and marketing bikes of staggering quality. Cyclists don't generally buy a handbuilt bike because it's lighter or faster; they buy it because it's designed and fabricated just for them.

This shift toward self-expression has also impacted other corners of bike culture. Think about the ways people dress while riding. Fashion and bike riding have collided in a big way, impacting both technical apparel and the ways in which people integrate nontechnical clothes into their riding lives. New and legacy brands have created entire categories of things people can wear on a bike and have radically expanded the offerings in existing categories. Dynamic shifts have been happening, are happening, and will continue to happen.

Rapha (see page 209) brought classy restraint and thoughtful colorways to technical clothes. Adaptations of that concept spread to mountain biking (and running). Giro introduced its New Road line for people who wanted technical clothes that looked more like regular clothes. Suddenly, a bunch of designers and brands began making jeans for people who ride. City dwellers, led mostly by young people and women, perhaps taking some cues from Europe, started riding to work, school, and the coffee shop in cool fashion. And all of these individual trends would inform a coherent, interconnected phenomenon.

There are, of course, still road-riding enthusiasts who dress like they and their mates are part of a racing club with an official uniform, while many folks who do lift-served riding still dress in high-vis colors and outfits with giant logos. In other words, some riders still wear the old uniforms, which is fine. But there are way more people than ever before who are doing their own thing, finding a style that matches their lifestyle. Bike-share programs like Citi Bike in New York have done a lot to normalize the idea of just riding in whatever you're wearing on a given day. Giro, with support from Canyon, SRAM, and other brands, recently founded an elite collective—in essence a team that participates in popular races and rides but whose goal is to advocate for inclusivity. And to that end, the Flashpoint MVMNT collective makes it clear that they are trying to prove that a uniform or specific look is not required to be accepted. That's an interesting way to sell apparel and gear.

People should just wear whatever the hell they want—whatever expresses who they want to be on a bike ride.

Like many other passionate road riders, I used to make fun of technical apparel made by Primal, famous for selling jerseys with huge Grateful Dead, Pink Floyd, army, and beer-inspired graphics. In a different era, these seemed cheesy, an insult to the Euro-styled class of road riding. Now this snobbery seems utterly ridiculous. And I think, in general, the polarity on this sort of thing is shifting within bike culture. People should just wear whatever the hell they want—whatever expresses who they want to be on a bike ride.

There is a media entity called Velominati. From the start, Velominati was a list that supposedly codified the rules of cycling—what to wear and how to set up your bike and how to behave to be a proper cyclist. If you were already experienced and secure within bike culture, it was easy to see the rules as a clever joke; if you were newer to cycling or outside mainstream roadie culture, the list could look like a confusing act of gatekeeping.

The rules became popular both because they were funny and because they curated the classic guidelines about etiquette and style within road-racing culture. But cycling culture can be painfully earnest sometimes, and eventually, a lot of people who see themselves as serious cyclists began to take the list too seriously. As if there really are rules governing what color bar tape you should use or when you can wear a cycling cap or what kind of gearing a road bike should have. The joke ceased to be funny.

In 2017, I penned an opinion piece expressing my frustrations with the rules and what they represent. I was tired of seeing so many cyclists telling other riders they were doing it wrong. Especially since we were—and remain—in an age in which most everyone wants bike culture to be more inclusive, it was disturbing that the criticism tended to be coming from experienced white guys. Soon thereafter, I coined a new slogan: "If you're riding a bike, you're doing it right." The idea is that the only rule—beyond don't be dangerous or a jerk—is that there are no rules.

This, to me, is the essence of the self-expression movement within bike culture. Wear what you want. Ride what and where and how you want. In the end, style is not about conforming to a code—it's about expressing your personality. And self-expression is ultimately about being true to yourself.

It's easy to talk about self-expression on a micro scale. In other words, to think about how riders embrace their own individuality.

But when you zoom out, the conversation about self-expression becomes a conversation about inclusivity and tolerance. On paper at least, many riders increasingly want bike culture to be the biggest possible tent—full of people who don't look like them or ride like them or come from similar circumstances. For this to succeed, experienced riders need to be more welcoming to people who are looking to enter that tent.

Communities that often are marginalized shouldn't feel pressure to conform to existing rules; they should just be met where they are and accepted. They need to feel confident that if they are riding a bike, they are doing it right. Because it's the truth.

Far too often when discussing the soul and personality of the bike-riding community, the conversation can wind up centered around what I'd call traditional road-riding culture. Whether it's unconscious or intentional, a lot of people imagine the culture as a pyramidic org chart with experienced road riders at the top. Certainly, a lot of those experienced road riders have long seen it that way. This is perhaps why so many people who didn't identify with this group but still felt passionate about riding bikes in some other way liked the idea of bike tribes or just were comfortable riding a lot without feeling like a part of something larger.

I don't actually think this group ever sat at the center of bike culture. I think they (along with mountain biking enthusiasts) have been the most important consumers for big companies in the bike industry. They have consumed a lot of content and purchased a lot of equipment and tend to come from privileged communities. So they sucked up most of the oxygen in the room.

On the bright side, I see a lot of positive change in how this spandex-wearing cohort looks at the rest of bike culture, and also how other riding communities look at the road-riding core. This development is closely tied to the growing interest in self-expression and inclusivity. Right now there are so many cool bike-riding cultures forming, growing, and morphing that are making ripples or waves outside their spaces. For instance, the so-called Bike Life movement. Created and sustained by urban riders who are Black or from other underrepresented communities, the movement empowers and celebrates folks to take over historically unfriendly city streets and ride with artistry, rebellion, athleticism, and an intense sense of community. Everybody who rides a bike knows deep down that doing wheelies is profoundly cool. Bike Life riders have created a vital riding scene in the most hostile of environments without conforming to cycling traditions, and they express themselves through riding in ways that have social, political, athletic, and artistic contexts. And because their talents are so well captured and conveyed through social media, millions of other people who ride have taken notice.

There is so much rad inspiration out there that is pushing the boundaries of what bike culture can encompass. Consider the example of Scottish trials rider Danny MacAskill, who has an immense talent not only for bike stunts but also for translating those skills to cinematic storytelling—his videos and short films

Riders are increasingly free to express themselves however they want. Shown here is the irrepressibly imaginative builder Dario Pegoretti, who sadly died in 2018.

Riders roll with great style on the Brooklyn Bridge. The so-called Bike Life movement has created a beautiful scene that is at once creative, inclusive, and rebellious.

collectively have been watched more than five hundred million times on YouTube alone. Of course, people love to gape at his amazing tricks, but I think they also love how his content has a sense of place, an air of wonderment, a highly artistic sense of style. His flair is undeniable.

In a similar vein, tens of millions of people around the world watch Red Bull Rampage, a freeride mountain bike event near Zion National Park in Utah, where riders descend a sprawling mesa however they choose, showing enormous skill, courage, and artistry. It's the only time in my life that I've seen someone roll off a 60-foot (18 m) climb and not only survive but earn style points along the way. So many people in the cycling community who don't do any aggressive gravity mountain biking watch Rampage because they grasp and admire the extraordinary expressiveness and technical skill of Rampage participants. The same increasingly can be said for elite women in the freeriding community who participated in Formation. A lot of riders who remember hucking a bike off the curb as a kid feel a kinship with the rarefied few who are skilled enough to gracefully huck off a cliff.

Thankfully, the inspirations are not restricted to riders who can do wheelies through traffic, launch from one building to another, or do high-amplitude backflips in the desert. There is this old chestnut in bike culture that the perfect number of bikes to own is N + 1—in other words, one more than you already have. In the past, there was a strong whiff of privilege to the joke—a celebration of material consumption—but more recently, I've seen riders buying bikes to try new disciplines or interests. It means that lines that used to separate riding subcultures are dissolving.

In recent years, nothing has been hotter than gravel riding, as riders seek new challenges and safer roads to ride and events that have a more laid-back, experiential quality than is typical on paved roads. Nearly everything—the gear, the clothing, the vibe, the competitiveness, even the party scene—about gravel is different from road riding, so now we have a big swath of riders who are getting a taste of a new idiosyncratic culture and liking it. It has even impacted pro cycling programs; consider how the professional team sponsored by EF Education has such a robust alternative racing schedule and is supporting many of its top riders in embracing the personality of the culture. Enthusiasts like pro athletes who drink beer with them.

Unlike gravel riding, urban riding on fixed-gear bikes is not a new fad; in fact, it's now an established scene that has been impacting the rest of bike culture for many years. For better or worse, the style, verve, attitude, and equipment from this world— once the province of bike messengers and alley cat devotees and folks who were real-life hipsters—have widely impacted many urban riders who still believe in gears and freewheels. In every big American city I visit, I see young people who have this effortlessly authentic bike identity. They are sort of like skateboarders in the sense that they are held together as a community by being distinctively individual.

Bike culture gets stronger and bigger when everyone who rides feels comfortable expressing their authentic self.

I could go on and on. There are the bikepackers, the BMXers, the fatbikers, the cyclocrossers, the alt-road wanderers, the nighttime social riders. The mountain bike space was never monolithic, but it keeps pushing outward. There is the ever-growing number of casual and utility riders in cities and small towns who have a style (or anti-style) that has changed how many of us ride to get a macchiato. There are just so many subcultures and kinds of riding and vernaculars of style that a vastly larger number of riders are realizing that they can curate a lifestyle and biking identity that is drawn from all over the culture.

Over the past decade, I've seen a dramatic shift in how bikes are perceived as they intersect with style, fashion, culture, art, community, and other elements of modern society. Now it's common to go into a cool boutique or a gourmet grocer and see a bicycle mounted on the wall or in a display case, because now bicycles connote the good life, an expression of something beautiful. They're in tons of fashion ads and editorial spreads because people associate bikes with personal style.

All of this is happening because people who ride care about how they express themselves. They feel something beautiful while riding a bike and want to reflect this back to the world. It's deeper than style or fashion, which already have substance. It's about how riders see themselves—the very core of their identity at times—and also the way they accept other people they interact with on the road. This self-expression is presently a big part of why I ride and why I love to ride. Perhaps you feel the same.

The elegantly simple answer to questions about why we ride is that it is a fun and meaningful way to transport ourselves to a better place.

Adam Myerson

A Bike Racer Who Stands Out for Being Himself and Fighting Injustice

Even now, Adam Myerson is surprised that bike racing became his thing. Growing up, he was a skate kid who didn't really dig team sports. He liked skate culture because it welcomed artfulness and radical inclusion. But it turned out that he ultimately didn't just like bike racing—he loved it so much that it became a through line in his life. So he set out to bring some artfulness and radical inclusion to bike racing.

Myerson grew up in Dorchester, Massachusetts. It was in many ways a challenging childhood—he remembers experiencing homelessness at times, he remembers the oven being open to heat the kitchen, he remembers his mom sending him to the door when workers came to turn off the utilities. He got serious about bikes when he was around fifteen. Before long, he saw bike racing as a way to get out of Dorchester—in a literal sense, to pedal to a more peaceful place beyond the city line, and in another as a tool to get him out permanently, to college and beyond. Myerson went to the University of Massachusetts at Amherst, where he earned a degree in English and won a collegiate national cyclocross championship in 1997.

Myerson does not look like a conventional clean-cut athlete. He has a lot of tattoos, a pierced septum, and stretched earlobes. He likes to joke that you can get a job at Starbucks looking like that now, but back when he was coming up in the sport, it was an issue.

Myerson was (and is) a sprinter and cyclocross specialist. He was committed to racing without doping. He obviously had talent but likely succeeded as a pro because of an obsession with racecraft, the art of reading a race. He looked like a punk rocker. He was outspoken about social issues, sexuality, culture. "All along, I had to be true to myself," Myerson says, acknowledging that the consequences of his life choices were more negative than positive until the social-media age. Even though he was winning races, certain opportunities never came along. He remembers trying to get on the prestigious Saturn Cycling Team— a squad repping a brand with the slogan "a different kind of car company"—in the '90s, but it seemed they didn't want racers who were quite so different or quite so strident about performance-enhancing drugs.

In the end, Myerson raced professionally for thirteen years. He never got to race in Europe at the highest level, but he was a force in the domestic scene, winning plenty of races—and doing it clean. And then, continuing to train and race hard, he went on to win a bunch of master's national championships in multiple disciplines.

But honestly, Myerson is not being profiled here because he won important bike races; rather, it's because of his unfiltered authenticity. The growth of social media gave Myerson a platform to share his views—on racing and doping, on a range of thorny social topics, on bike advocacy issues—giving bike culture access to a racer who was way more outspoken and open than most. He also got increasingly active as a coach, race organizer, and board member of various governing bodies in the sport, all efforts that were focused on helping young or amateur riders. Myerson has been tireless in speaking out on behalf of inclusion, clean sport, and social justice.

In particular, Myerson has worked with more than a few transgender racers—coaching, training, and advising them—as well as watching the work they put into the sport and the constant friction they face. There may be no one in bike racing who has more practical experience or hard data related to the physiological realities of trans racers. And he's fought hard to advocate for their safety and well-being—and their humanity—within his leadership and advisory roles with governing bodies and event organizers. This advocacy has gotten considerably more challenging as anti-trans legislation gets more common and as trans athletes increasingly face troubling new restrictions that threaten their access to participate in sports.

Myerson turned fifty in 2022. He's married, with a young son. He's still racing in age-group national championships. His coaching business, Cycle-Smart, takes up a lot of his time. He coaches a ton of promising juniors, some of whom will go on to be professional racers. Others will wash out of the sport before they're done with college. "With all my juniors, I focus on how racing bikes can make their lives better—I care more about that than about results," he says. Bike racing has changed since Myerson was a teenager—it's much more data driven, where the quantified size of a rider's engine and their watts per kilogram are prioritized over racecraft. He believes in the adage "all bodies on bikes," and this means that as a coach to juniors, he must protect some racers from eating disorders rather than push them to win.

Things have a way of working out. He had a rough childhood, and charting his own uncompromising path limited his opportunities, but now Myerson is in a good place. "I've never done anything that made me feel happy like being in the middle of a bike race," he says, which is a good thing because he's done thousands of bike races and is still rubbing elbows at speed. He's coaching young talent, speaking out about the injustices faced by many marginalized communities, and engaging in bike advocacy in Boston. Big brands like Bianchi and Factor have sponsored him, and he feels like his only responsibility as a brand ambassador is to be himself 24/7. "I'm finally getting paid to be myself," he says.

Myerson knows that all the major social issues of our time intersect with bike culture and has tirelessly used his platform to advocate for positive change.

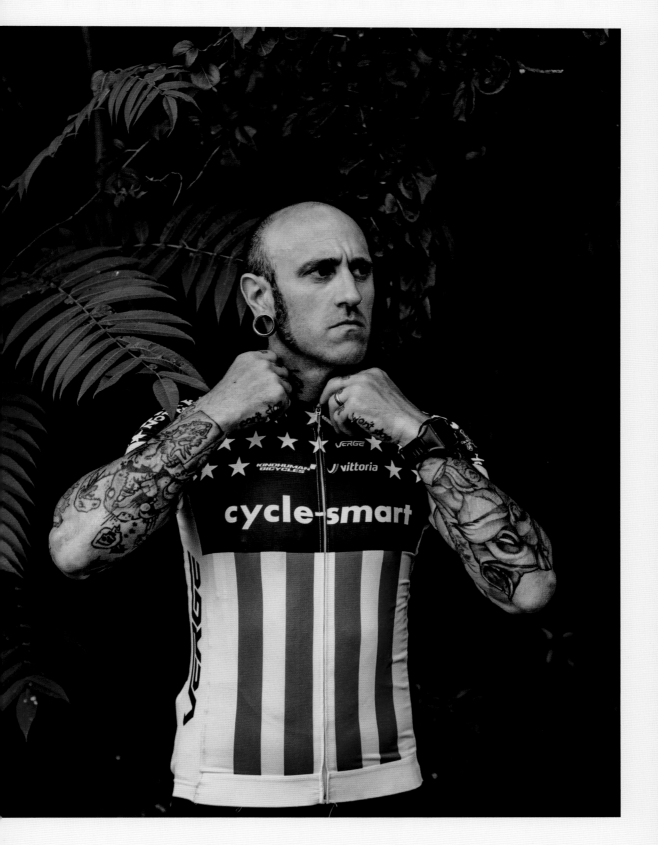

Richard Sachs

Portrait of an artist

Richard Sachs, the grand master of American framebuilding, who has been building bicycles for five decades, is reluctant to call his work art. Instead, he sees bicycles as appliances and views his craft as a trade, dismissing framebuilders who discuss self-expression as "self-indulgent." Sachs says he finds no inspiration within the bike industry, calling it "kind of staid and boring."

But when he pivots to where he *does* find inspiration, the contours of what makes Sachs and his frames interesting come into focus. He discusses *The Soul of a Tree*, the memoir of George Nakashima, and how the midcentury furniture maker was utterly attuned to his materials. Sachs extols the work of watchmaker Philippe Dufour, who produces every part of his watches by hand and is obsessive about the smallest details. And he admits that when he's in a rut, he rewatches *Jiro Dreams of Sushi*, the 2011 documentary about an eighty-five-year-old sushi master who remains singularly focused on the pursuit of perfection.

Sachs didn't set out to build bikes. He applied to become an apprentice in England in the early 1970s after his attempts to get a writing job failed. He sent about thirty letters asking "to observe and be a gopher" to English bikebuilders and received only one yes, from Witcomb in South London. This changed the arc of his life. Sachs came back to the States and in 1975 opened his own business in Connecticut. Since then, he has handcrafted thousands of lugged steel bicycles.

In interviews, Sachs often acknowledges that mass-produced modern race bikes are of very high quality. "They may all look the same, like they popped out of a waffle iron, but they are well designed and proven in top races," he says. But still, he expresses sadness about how the digital age and global economy have altered how bicycles are made. "Now someone models an art file and sends it to Asia, and a final thing gets shipped back in a container."

The grand master understands why customers pay thousands and wait years for a Richard Sachs frameset—not for the bike so much as for what went into the bike. "I have a relationship with my materials and tools," he says. "It is an art to take a pile of materials and use tools to transform it into something functional and beautiful."

An already heavy conversation gets weightier when I ask Sachs about Dario Pegoretti (see page 177). The two men were friends and collaborators for decades. On paper, they seemed different—Pegoretti could be flamboyant and made bikes with wild paint jobs, while Sachs crafts meticulous lugged frames—but they shared an uncompromising dedication to the pursuit of excellence and a mastery of geometry and metal. "Dario was the only one who truly understood me," Sachs says.

So Sachs pushes on alone, still wrestling to understand the meaning of his devotion to his craft while obsessively seeking communion with it. "It's like surfing," Sachs says with a laugh. "I'm always out there, looking for the next wave."

Molly Cameron

A pioneer for transgender athletes

Molly Cameron is variously known as a veteran elite bike racer, bike shop owner, content maker, sports-marketing and sports-management professional, and transgender advocate. She has been racing her bike and speaking truth to power for a few decades now. The waters have been choppy for a long time, and she is understandably weary—as well as understandably hopeful and frightened. For queer and nonbinary and transgender athletes, this too often is the world they ride in.

Cameron has been out as a transgender woman for more than twenty years. She was the first transgender woman to participate in a men's UCI Cyclocross World Cup race. She has raced in women's fields and men's fields and has spent a quarter century dealing with the exhausting experience that trans and nonbinary riders face every time they seek the communion and challenge of competition: the endless questions about their identity and fairness.

"Identity and self-expression are front and center in everything I do," Cameron says. And it's true. We're living through a pivotal moment in time, when transgender people in the bike community are navigating through frightening obstacles—including tough restrictions from governing bodies and the passage of anti-trans laws in some US states that further marginalize trans women and threaten their access to sports.

Cameron admits that she's an "anti-capitalist capitalist." Meaning she's trying to work within the system to help fix it. In 2021, Cameron founded an advocacy organization called Riders Inspiring Diversity & Equality. Catalyzed by the wave of legislation targeting trans athletes and others who are LGBTQIA+, RIDE is focused on nonperformative action to preserve access to health care and scholastic sports—and other fundamental freedoms—for folks in these marginalized groups. "I am more than willing to put myself out there on these issues so other people don't have to go through this," Cameron says.

As an elite rider and advocate sponsored by brands like Shimano, Cameron does her most effective work just by being a genuine part of the bike-racing community—and by relentlessly making the case that tolerance and diversity and forward thinking on social issues are good for business. "The bike industry has long said they want *everyone* on bikes," she says.

Cameron admits that she's never felt entirely welcome in bike culture. She's experienced that feeling of walking into a bike shop or visiting the offices of a big bike brand and seeing no visible signs of queer or trans people. She's seen recreational athletes who are simply trying to enjoy sport like anyone else get bullied at races. But she also sees signs that things are improving. She recalls her last trip to the Sea Otter Classic—a popular bike celebration, racing event, and trade show held near Monterey, California, that has long been a "festival of bro culture"—and seeing progress for the first time. "I saw a lot of queer and trans folks, people of color, and women working at brands," she says. "And not just the little punk rock brands; the bigger ones. That's great—I felt more comfortable than I've ever felt before."

The fight against ignorance and hate and discrimination will not be easy. Cameron knows that. But she also knows that bike culture is open to change. "Bikes saved my life," she says. "I was struggling with sexual identity and gender, and bikes helped me through it. Cycling really attracts the weirdos. It's beautiful in that way. There's so much room for expression with bikes. There's not one way to do it."

Don Walker

Launching NAHBS and a resurgence of handbuilt bikes

It was 2004, and some of the best framebuilders in America, lifers like Richard Sachs and Brian Baylis, enjoyed an ongoing chat on a message board. Now and again, someone would float the idea of getting everyone together in person to share information and socialize. But no one really did anything about it.

Then Don Walker, a builder who lived in Hewitt, Texas, at the time, made that leap. In January 2005, roughly forty builders gathered at a Sheraton in the Houston suburbs, giving birth to the North American Handmade Bicycle Show.

Potential customers were welcome to come—and some hard-core enthusiasts did attend—but the focus at first was for the framebuilders themselves. There were seminars on tubing, lug carving, and tooling for advanced builders to swap ideas and amateurs to raise their game.

"People really wanted to get together," says Walker, who is now based in Georgia. "It wasn't just about what was on the show floor." It still makes him smile to remember how the bar at the Sheraton ran out of beer on Saturday night.

From that humble, raucous beginning, NAHBS (pronounced "nabs") grew to become an influential consumer-facing institution. Walker said it really took off at the 2008 show in bike-crazy Portland, Oregon, which featured more than 150 exhibitors and drew more than 7,000 paid visitors. Walker moved NAHBS every year or two—Indianapolis, Richmond, and Austin came next—and the show's importance kept growing. The interest in bespoke bicycles, which had been an extremely niche category only a decade earlier, was suddenly a broad phenomenon.

When asked to explain why his show—and the builders who participated—enjoyed a boom in this era, Walker cites two unrelated factors. He thinks that a lot of bike enthusiasts who became passionate about the sport and riding during the Lance Armstrong era got cynical about the big brands that sponsored racers during that time frame. But more important, he says, is that people connected to the passion of the builders and the unique qualities of their bikes. "In general, framebuilding is a horrible way to make a living, and you're only going to do it seriously for a long time if you have a deep passion for cycling," he says. Walker himself transitioned from working on aircraft to building track bikes decades ago and has never looked back.

Alas, NAHBS was unable to survive a hiatus begun by Covid. In 2023, the handbuilt community got a replacement of sorts with the MADE bike show, which debuted in Portland, Oregon. Walker's creation is no longer with us, but the central mission of that enterprise—to bring the builder community and the people who adore their bikes together—lives on and thrives.

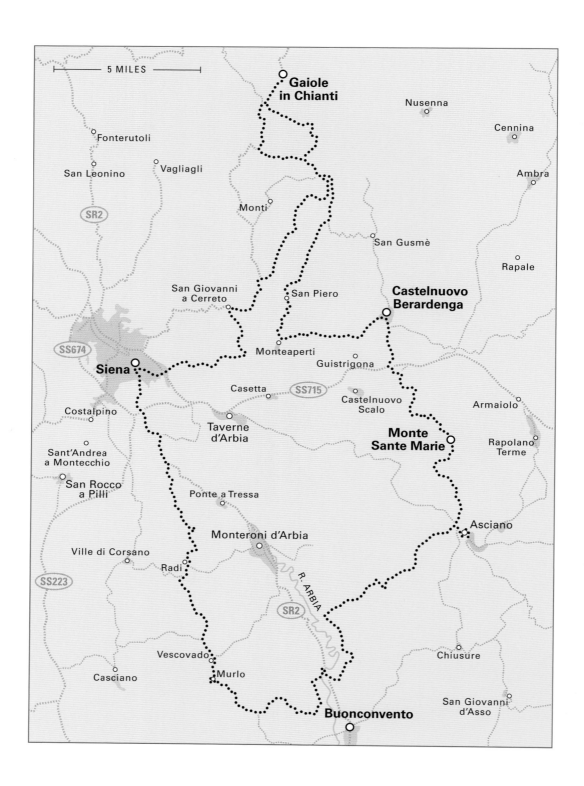

Live to Ride

L'Eroica Medio

In Tuscany, a ruggedly artful celebration of the sport's heritage

BY THE NUMBERS

· *84 miles (135 km)*

· *7,280 feet (2,200 m)
  elevation gain*

· *Total of strade bianche:
  36 miles (58 km)*

There are few places in the world that can stake a claim as a spiritual heartland of cycling tradition—the Chianti region of Italy is one of them. As a beautiful homage to the heritage of riding culture, an event called L'Eroica (The Heroic) was created to give contemporary riders a taste of how the sport used to be.

First held in 1997, the event sends riders onto the famed strade bianche—the old white sandy roads that dot the Tuscan hillsides (and eventually inspired a pro bike race with that name). While participants at nearly every other long-distance event wear modern technical apparel and ride state-of-the-art bicycles, at L'Eroica, riders honor the old days by riding antique steel bikes and wearing relatively period-correct kits made from wool. But rather than being some cheesy costume party, L'Eroica captures the pageantry and expressive beauty of road riding in another era. For more than twenty years, the event has offered multiple routes. The medium— or medio—route is a doable challenge for fit amateurs.

• The event starts and ends in Gaiole, a charming village located between Florence and Siena. About 20 miles (32 km) from the start, the mostly rural route edges into denser civilization in Siena. Riders pedal into and out of the famed Palazzo Pubblico, a nine-hundred-year-old gothic plaza where the dramatic finish of the Strade Bianche professional bike race takes place.

• Roughly 40 miles (64 km) into the route, riders pass through Buonconvento, a small historic walled city.

• About 54 miles (87 km) in, riders face the Monte Sante Marie, the toughest climb on the route. The 7-mile (11 km) climb, entirely on dirt, has a vertical gain of 1,263 feet (385 m) and several pitches topping a 12 percent grade.

• The 65-mile (105 km) point offers the route's final food stop in Castelnuovo Berardenga, an atmospheric small town with churches dating back to the seventh century.

• Near the 70-mile (113 km) mark, riders must tackle a long and undulating 6-mile (10 km) climb. Thankfully, most of it is paved.

Riding Eroica can be very hard, but the event has elevated interest in the beauty of vintage equipment and the elegance of the sport's early days.

Pashley Guv'nor

Obsessive craft in the service of unapologetic joy

An elegant contemporary revival of a 1930s race bike, the Guv'nor is not a bike built for some obvious practical use. It evokes passion more than purpose. The frame, which has classic lines and proportions, is fabricated from Reynolds 531 steel, a legendary material from another age. The bike oozes simple elegance, but the specifications telegraph an obsessive attention to detail. Gold-lined rims with stainless steel spokes. A swept handlebar with hand-sewn leather grips. A brass bell. A Brooks leather saddle with titanium rims. You're not going to buy this because you want to ride faster—you'll buy it because it makes your heart beat faster.

Pegoretti Responsorium

A handbuilt beauty that is Dario Pegoretti's legacy

When it comes to handbuilt bikes, there are enough glorious options to fill an entire book. Bikes with meticulous technique and artistry, boutique materials, masterful paint jobs—all sized and built to bring joy, comfort, and performance to one person. Still, when it comes to the emotional resonance of a custom bike, it's hard to top a bike from the workshop of the late Dario Pegoretti. His disciples have carried his legacy onward in Verona, Italy, where steel and aluminum bikes with old-world class and craftsmanship and new-world vitality continue to be built. The Responsorium, made from Columbus stainless-steel XCR tubing and painted with punkish fine-art verve, is a thing of beauty and a machine built for all-day rides in the toughest conditions.

BikeID Step-Through

A city bike that is a rideable object of desire

There's no crime in buying a bicycle as a fashion accessory—something that gets you around town in style. This chromed-out beauty from BikeID has thoughtful touches—stainless steel fenders and basket, a leather Brooks saddle and leather grips, an internal seven-speed hub, both coaster and conventional brakes. The bike is comfortable and capable in the city, and don't worry if some people ogle it at the coffee shop.

Big Flyer 29"

The bike that defines wheelie culture

It's an icon in the so-called Bike Life scene—an urban-riding culture defined by wheelies, artistry, rebellion, self-expression, and community. Made by SE Bikes, a storied BMX brand that has been around since the 1970s, the Big Flyer 29" is spec'd for the wheelie lifestyle. It has a lightweight aluminum frame; a durable chromoly fork; wide and grippy tires; wheelie pegs; a sealed rear hub; and little touches that capture the vibe of the scene. Fittingly, it comes in a wide range of colorways, giving riders lots of options to express their style.

Paul Smith Cycling Jerseys

Fashion can't intersect with performance any better than this.

The collision of fashion with technical cycling apparel has more than a decade of momentum, but the offerings keep improving. British designer Paul Smith, himself a dedicated rider, continues to churn out some inspired looks for both the spandex set and those who want to walk from the bike rack to the meeting room. These short-sleeve jerseys, made in Italy from a lightweight and recycled poly blend, offer UV protection and excellent breathability. The designs will surely change from season to season, but the cheerful, colorful fashion-forward vibe will carry on.

Chris King R45 Hubs

Who says bicycle hubs can't be sexy?

You wouldn't buy these hubs simply because they look rad and come in many cool colors, but their amazing aesthetics sure make the decision easier. Built around Chris King's legendary made-in-house bearings—surgical-grade steel or ceramic, your call—and a lightweight body, these hubs will roll better and last longer than almost any others you can buy. You will feel and hear the quality on every ride—just as you will admire the stunning colors and finish of these hubs. They are an extremely classy way to add some flair to your ride.

How Rapha brought fashion to mainstream cycling culture

The Rapha brand and the movement it begat were born out of frustration. It was 2003, and Lance Armstrong had already made the proclamation that it's not about the bike—but Simon Mottram and Luke Scheybeler disagreed. For a lot of riders, it *was* about the bike. "We saw how people felt that the bikes were beautiful objects," Scheybeler says. "But we also saw that the clothing options were terrible, that people were going out riding dressed like Power Rangers."

Mottram was the more visible face of the Rapha brand, managing finances, PR, and day-to-day operations, while Scheybeler (who later also cofounded the running apparel brand Tracksmith) worked behind the scenes on design, branding, and marketing. A year before Rapha officially launched with a strikingly simple black jersey with a single white stripe on the left sleeve, the two men scoured books about cycling history, looking for inspiration. "From the start, our goal was to make the brand about emotional appeal," Scheybeler says. "It was never about selling clothing that would make you faster."

They wound up settling on the imagery and vibe of the 1950s through the '70s—a golden age in cycling when the heroes of the sport had movie-star energy and wore kits with a kind of simple elegance. Down the road, Rapha and its numerous imitators would turn to Pantone trends to create fashion-forward colorways, but at the start, Scheybeler says, he was more inspired and guided by photography that was used in Calvin Klein and Armani campaigns in the '80s. He and Mottram settled on making apparel items

Rapha had an influential impact on bike culture by bringing a classic fashion sense to technical cycling apparel that many brands have since copied.

with a basic look, high-end textiles, and one asymmetric detail. They thought that yellow, the iconic hue of the Tour de France, was too obvious, so they gravitated toward pink as their signature accent color.

In the early years, Rapha's marketing leaned heavily on black-and-white photography and cinematic videos that evoked the beauty of suffering on the bike. Their models—in a later era they might be called influencers—rarely wore sunglasses or a helmet. "We caught some shit for that," Scheybeler says. "But we wanted people to look into the souls of these riders." Though the campaign was arguably a bit pretentious, it was effective. "We pulled back on it later on out of necessity," Scheybeler says. "But it was a pretty strong metaphor for life and for riding—the more you put into it, the more you get out of it."

Ultimately, the Rapha brand succeeded on many levels. Mottram, Scheybeler, and their team wound up creating a multifaceted luxury/high-performance brand, selling cycling kits, lifestyle apparel, shoes, and striking accessories, and also operating a successful chain of cycling clubs in Europe and North America. They sponsored and outfitted pro teams at the highest level of the sport. They collaborated with a huge range of artists, designers, and brands. And in 2017, bike-obsessed Walmart heirs Steuart and Tom Walton purchased a majority interest in Rapha for $260 million.

Two decades after the brand was born, the frustration that launched Rapha has brought an influential and widely copied fashion sensibility to road-cycling apparel. In many privileged corners of bike culture, it's common to see hordes of riders wearing a stylishly anonymous kit like it's a uniform. Scheybeler, who's no longer associated with the brand, sees that, too, as well as some Rapha pro kits that he thinks look "a bit obvious, with this OCD slickness." But he understands that fashion is an ever-evolving beast, and he hopes to see style cues from gravel riding, camping, and hiking picked up in cycling apparel. "Maybe it needs a bit of a shake-up," he says. "But in the end, we created a beautiful blank slate that you can add to. The greats have always found ways to add flair to their kit."

Rapha's early marketing campaigns featured black-and-white photography that theatrically celebrated suffering and the heritage of the sport.

Everyone who pedals a bike, whether they're pushing their physical limits in wild places or running errands around town, is united by a love of the transformational power of riding.

Riders don't just want to see nature—we want to feel connected to the natural world.

PHOTO CREDITS

INDEX

Fausto Coppi, shown here at the 1951 Giro d'Italia, could do many things with unmistakable verve.